stasi eldredge

beautiful me

believing God's truth about you

transforming lives together

BEAUTIFUL ME
Published by David C Cook
4050 Lee Vance Drive
Colorado Springs, CO 80918 U.S.A.

Integrity Music Limited, a Division of David C Cook
Brighton, East Sussex BN1 2RE, England

The graphic circle C logo is a registered trademark of David C Cook.

LCCN 2015944608
ISBN 978-1-4347-0994-3
eISBN 978-1-4347-1012-3

© 2016 Stasi Eldredge
Published in association with Yates & Yates, www.yates2.com

The Team: Alice Crider, Elisa Stanford, Amy Konyndyk,
Helen Macdonald, Susan Murdock
Cover Design: Nick Lee

Printed in the United States of America
First Edition 2016

2 3 4 5 6 7 8 9 10 11

041019

To Abigail, Gracelyn Rose, and Hartley Faye
With love, joy, faith, and true
hope from your auntie.

contents

welcome!

I'm glad you're here! I'm Stasi, and it's true that most people wouldn't consider me a young woman anymore. I'm in my fifties. We might as well get that out in the open right away. But I've learned some things along the way, getting to this age. I've learned from the women around me—younger and older. One of the greatest things I've learned so far in my life is the value of time spent alone with God.

Does that sound strange? How do we go about being alone with God?

The incredible truth is that the God of the universe wants you to talk with him. To turn to him every day. To listen to him through Scripture, silence, and the words of others who know him.

Each day in this three-month devotional includes a Bible verse, a word of encouragement from me, and then a prayer, question, or declaration for you to use as a starting point for your own intimate time with God.

A lot of people like to spend their devotional time in the morning, but others prefer that intentional time with God just before bed. You can experiment with what time and place works best for you. A coffee shop? Between classes? Just before you head to your job?

The important thing to know is that God wants to meet with you even more than you want to meet with him! He wants you to know him and know how much he values you. Wherever and whenever you grab this book, know that God is waiting to speak words of love to you. He is eager to tell you, again and again, that you are beautiful. Right here. Right now. Are you ready?

1

beautiful you!

There has never been the slightest doubt in my mind that the God who started this great work in you would keep at it and bring it to a flourishing finish on the very day Christ Jesus appears.

—Philippians 1:6 MSG

Did you know you are beautiful? Not just pretty or cute or acceptable, but *beautiful*. Beyond measure. Beyond anything else God created. I know you don't always feel beautiful. I struggle with that too. But God sees us as beautiful, radiant, gifted, valued, and loved. I'm excited to think of you receiving that truth in your mind and spirit now, as a young woman, so that you can live out your beauty and your gifts throughout your lifetime!

That reminds me of a secret I want to share with you: life gets better. No, really. It does. It might feel hard for a while there. Life is kind of like that, but cross my heart, I'm telling you the truth. It gets better.

You will find your way. You will grow and learn and figure it out and change in the ways you so long to. Because of Jesus. Because of Jesus, change is not only possible but it's promised.

You are being transformed into the very image of Jesus. He who has called you is faithful, and what he has begun he will complete. You have a part to play too in God's work in you, and God will guide you in what that looks like. Jesus wants you to be free to be who you are! Beautiful, beautiful *you*. And that's no secret.

Jesus, you are transforming me into your image. What part do you want me to play in that transformation today? Show me how you want me to see you. Show me how you want me to see myself! In Jesus's name, amen.

2

God made you *you*

For you created my inmost being;
you knit me together in my mother's womb.
I praise you because I am fearfully and wonderfully made;
your works are wonderful,
I know that full well.

—Psalm 139:13–14

Self-assured is not how anyone would have described me in high school. I may have looked that way. I sure tried hard to appear that way. But if there had been a sign hanging over my heart, it would have read, "Just tell me who I'm supposed to be and I'll be that." My parents had an idea of who I was supposed to be. (Smarter! Thinner! More popular!) My friends were quite willing to tell me, without even speaking, who I was supposed to be. (Funnier! Prettier!) I let my sisters tell me who I was supposed to be. I sure let boys tell me.

I let other people tell me who I was and who I was not before I even had a clue as to whether or not they were right.

Maybe we come into this world with a grand sense of self. But then life chips away at our innate sense of unique well-being. Life happens, things happen, words are spoken, and it isn't very long before we figure out that in order to survive, there is a person we need to be, and she isn't us. Not truly. Not fully. Not freely.

Just tell me who I am supposed to be and I'll be that.

Big sigh.

So I bet you can guess what I'm going to say next, right? I'm going to tell you that in order to have a life worth living, you need to be you! You're correct.

In order to have a life worth living, you need to be you. Not the friend-dictated version. Not the Internet-updated version. But the true version.

You are you. You actually can't be anyone else—that's why it's so exhausting and unsatisfying to pretend. God made you *you* on purpose. You are the only one alive who ever was or ever will be you. You is not only who you get to be; it's who you are supposed to be. Let me tell you, being yourself is a lot less work than trying to be someone else. I know because I've tried it both ways! It brings a lot more joy too. And that's a gift from God.

Jesus, I want to be who you created me to be. You made me on purpose. Help me to celebrate this every day!

3

---

well on your way

*I'm not saying that I have this all together, that I have
it made. But I am well on my way, reaching out for
Christ, who has so wondrously reached out for me.*
—Philippians 3:12 MSG

A lot of life's problems come when we would rather be
someone else. Anyone else. Sometimes others don't like us.
Sometimes we don't like ourselves. We know where we are
struggling or failing or hurting or simply wanting out. We
know we are not all that we are meant to be.

The very fact that we long for the change we do is a sign
that we are meant to have it. Our dissatisfaction with our
weaknesses and struggles points to the reality that continu-
ing to live in them is not our destiny.

That's what life is all about. Moving forward and upward
and becoming the next higher version of yourself, always.

But not merely by your own efforts. Not by a strength of will or a bitter form of self-discipline or a rigorous regime of self-loathing. But through the love of God.

I want to grow. I want to change. I want to become more true, more loving, more authentic, more me. Jesus wants that too. And he wants *you* to become more you too! Jesus loves who you are. He sees you and knows you and thinks you're amazing. He also knows who you are meant to be, and by his love and grace he wants to partner with you on your journey.

What words would you use to describe the true you?

4

pictures in the clouds

The joy of the LORD is your strength.
—Nehemiah 8:10

Do you ever feel as if you want more? More joy. More freedom. More hope. More healing. More life! You want to laugh more and be more kind. More happy. More yourself. You want to love more, know God more, and become more content in your own skin.

There is such a thing as holy dissatisfaction. It is an unsettled feeling inside that moves you not toward self-contempt but to a passionate pursuit of the God who says more is available.

I want more. I bet you do too. And God wants us to have that "more" most of all! What a great gift that he lets us delight in the things he wants us to have.

So go ahead and be smart. Be strong. Be kind. Be glorious. Be courageous. Be *you*. Care for your heart. Care for your body. Allow yourself to dream. Ask questions. Break barriers. Pursue truth. Pursue healing. Pursue Jesus.

Laugh. Explore. Pay more attention to how you feel than how you look. Tell yourself you're beautiful. Go for a walk. Daydream. Take a self-defense course. Volunteer. Be an advocate for someone in need. Find your passion. Read a book just for fun. Pray. Listen.

Find pictures in clouds. Laugh at yourself. Smile at strangers. Give large tips. Open the door for others. Say thank you when someone does it for you. Just say thank you. A lot. Respect your intuition. Practice a firm handshake. Look people in the eyes.

Ask God to reveal his love for you. Pay attention. Forgive offenses. Let people go who aren't true friends. Don't look back. Try something new. Get a bike. Pet a dog. Set a goal. Go bowling. Go to the zoo. Fly a kite at the park. Invite someone to come along with you.

When you enjoy something, be it a fragrance, a feeling, or a view, receive it as the love note from Jesus that it is and say to him, "I love you too."

Jesus, thank you for the good gifts you offer me today! I love _____ *about today.* [What are some things, even small things, that bring you joy on an ordinary day?] *And I want to say that I love you too!*

5

your most important journey

I have loved you with an everlasting love;
I have drawn you with unfailing kindness.

—Jeremiah 31:3

I used to think the journey of my life was about getting my act together, blowing it less frequently, and being a good girl. Serving people. Obeying. Following the rules. I thought that's what mattered most to God. Boy, was I wrong. What matters most to God is the heart.

Life is a journey of becoming the true you. Which means it is a journey of the heart. We have to begin with the heart because that is where all the true action is. Your heart is central. It's been battered, and there will be times when it will be battered again. It can cause you great pain and can get you into even greater trouble. You'll be tempted to lock it away, put it on a shelf, numb it, or maybe even kill it. Certainly, there will be times when you lose it. But the thing is, you can't truly live without your heart. And you are meant to live.

Your heart is, in fact, the most important thing about you. Your heart is also the most important thing to God. And that's really good news! Jesus came for your heart. To ransom, rescue, and restore the true you. He hasn't been moving heaven and earth through all eternity so that you would behave yourself. Fit into the crowd. Mind your manners. No. He wants to woo and win your heart for himself so that you will love him with it and live your life from it.

So we don't have to be perfect to follow God? Right. That's not just good news. That's *crazy* good news!

Jesus, woo my heart today! I want to fall in love with you.

6

---

where Christ dwells

Above all else, guard your heart,
for everything you do flows from it.
—Proverbs 4:23

Above all else, we are told, guard your heart. And guard not like a watchdog, fearfully keeping it in line, but guard as in tend, protect, and nurture. Most of us don't do that. Most of us watch what we look like more closely than we watch our hearts. And that is not a wise thing to do, because a life without heart is not worth living, and your life matters. Your heart matters.

Above all else, watch over your heart. Seriously? Why? Because you are made in the image of the Trinity! Have you ever wondered, *Where is that image?*

You are made in the image of God in your whole being but primarily in your heart. You have been created female by

23

God's design. It's his intention that you carry his image to the world as a woman. He created your feminine heart with the greatest of all possible dignities—as a reflection of God's own heart. In other words, you are feminine to the very core of your being.

And that is what Jesus has come to restore.

So when I speak about the heart, I am not speaking about your feelings, your emotions. You do feel deeply with the heart, but you think deeply there as well. When I speak of the heart, I am talking about the place where Christ dwells in you, by faith. The center of you. The core place inside where you are your most true self. That's what God tells us to guard—because it is so precious, so valuable, and so true to who you really are.

Jesus, I want to guard my heart. I want to see it as precious and beautiful. In my relationships, in my thoughts, in my dreams, help me keep my heart guarded for you.

7

---

loving yourself

Love your neighbor as yourself.
—Mark 12:33

When you become a Christian, you get a new heart. As believers with new hearts, we still struggle with sin. Yes. We are called to crucify our flesh every day. But we are not called to crucify our heart. We are called to guard it.

So this is what we know:

Your heart matters most to God.
Your heart needs protecting.
You need to be nice to it.

We can be so mean to ourselves, can't we? We say things to ourselves that we would never say to another human being. We can be harsh. (We see our flaws clearly, but it's much more difficult to see our goodness, right?) Here's the thing: You need to be kind to yourself so that you will be kind to others. Because the way you treat your heart is the way you will treat everyone else's. That's how it works.

So how are you doing today? How's your heart? How are you treating your heart? Are you being kind, encouraging, and loving to yourself? Jesus wants you to be. We are commanded to love our neighbors *as ourselves*. The thing is, we will. We will love others as we love ourselves. So if we are harsh to ourselves, we will be harsh to others whether we want to be or not. It will leak out.

Jesus loves you. He thinks you're worth protecting, pursuing, guarding, investing in, and giving his life for. He wants you to love you too. You still have areas in your life that you want to change. But just as you look for those you love to grow in certain areas, you can look for changes in yourself while at the same time loving who you are.

Jesus, thank you for my life. Help me learn to love myself. You created me with purpose. You love me with abundance. I receive that love!

the heart of the matter

And I will give you a new heart, and I will put a
new spirit in you. I will take out your stony, stubborn
heart and give you a tender, responsive heart.

—Ezekiel 36:26 NLT

You may have been taught that the heart is deceitfully wicked. Aren't our worldly desires wrong? It's true that the heart is wicked before salvation. But when a person believes in her heart that Jesus is the Son of God who came to save her and she surrenders herself to God, giving him his rightful place in her heart, she gets a new one!

See, God knows where the problems lie, and he has come to deal with them. He knows we need his help to live well and to love well. He knows our fallen hearts are deceitfully wicked, and he made arrangements, through Jesus Christ, for them to not stay that way.

I recently had the honor and the sorrow of being at the memorial service for my friend's twenty-four-year-old son. The service was holy. And I do mean *holy*. Grieving his passing. Celebrating his life. Thanking God for the truth that there is a day coming when all will be restored. No more good-byes. Ever.

At his service, nothing was shared about how he did or did not pick up his room. If he made his bed. Put his clothes away. Nothing about how old he was when he got his driver's license. Not a word about his grades, his roles, or his titles.

What people shared was how they felt in his presence. They shared stories about his sense of humor. Words flowed about how he *loved* people, about how he lived passionately from his heart, and about the joy he brought by being and offering his unique, quirky, imperfect, wonderful, on-the-road self.

It was his heart that mattered. And it's yours that matters too.

Jesus, you have given me a new heart. You have put a new spirit in me! You have taken out my stony, stubborn heart and given me a tender, responsive heart. I am so very thankful!

9
_____

wonder years?

Do you not know?
Have you not heard?
The LORD is the everlasting God,
the Creator of the ends of the earth.
He will not grow tired or weary,
and his understanding no one can fathom.
—Isaiah 40:28

Did you know that as a teenager, you actually feel things more strongly than adults do? It's true. Joy, sorrow, loss, heartbreak—your emotions run deep. That's also why there's really no such thing as "puppy love." First love is intense. (That's one of the reasons you want to guard your heart!)

As your hormonal levels change and spike, it can be a challenge for your skin to keep up with it all. Also, boys are suddenly much more interesting. Passing glances or a simple brush against an arm can make your stomach lurch. In a good way. Relationships with other girls can feel much more difficult, and their opinions seem much more weighty. Changeable too. Your friendships can become tricky. Adults can seem more stupid. Your mother more irritating. Your family more embarrassing.

It's normal.

Really.

It will pass.

It's also the season of life when you are more likely to take risks that later you wish you hadn't. Your biochemistry is changing. Some days you may just want to sit this "season" out, but you don't get to.

Well, maybe you can for an afternoon or even a week, but not for long. It's actually one of the most fabulous times of your one wild and precious life.

How you feel, what you think, what you experience, and the choices you make in this season matter. Today. Now. Always. You matter. These may not feel like "wonder years" or anything close to the best time of your life, but it is still your life. And God is with you—understanding and loving you through it all.

How does this season of life affect how you see yourself? Others? God?

10

the secret

This is the secret: Christ lives in you. This
gives you assurance of sharing his glory.
—Colossians 1:27 NLT

The paradox of change is that it involves surrendering ourselves to God, giving everything over to him—including all our efforts to change and all our resignation that we'll never change.

Then God restores us—the real us. Once we surrender ourselves, he gives us back our true selves. In fact, the most important journey any person will take is the journey into becoming herself through the love of God. It is a journey that will require courage, faith, and above all a willingness to grow and to let go. The journey of becoming is one of increased self-awareness coupled with a surrender of self. It is a dance between choosing and yielding, desiring and relinquishing, trying and giving up.

It is a beautiful paradox that the more God's we become, the more ourselves we become—the self he had in mind when he thought of you before the creation of the world. She's in there, girls. She might be badly bruised and covered with all sorts of muck, but she's in there. And Jesus comes to call her out.

What kind of person do you want to become? What do you want to be like? Ask God to breathe hope into your heart that you can become her.

11

---

an inside-out process

I have been crucified with Christ and I no longer live, but Christ lives in me.

—Galatians 2:20

In this process of becoming who God created us to be, we need to remember that shame and discipline are not agents of lasting change.

By shame, I mean a conversation with yourself in which you berate yourself for not being or doing what you consider to be the right thing. Like a shot of caffeine in the morning, shame may propel us onto the road of change, but we will find that hatred of self only leads us onto a never-ending roundabout.

Self-discipline isn't going to cut it either. Discipline, particularly spiritual discipline, is a holy and good thing, one that increases over a lifetime of practice. But when we lean on it alone to bring about the change we long for, we find that the fruit is *not* a grace-filled woman. We get angry. We get discouraged. Trying, striving, working harder may get us through the week, but it won't take us through the decades.

True transformation cannot be forced from the outside. It's an inside-out process. Have you ever created or received a list of ways to live, eat, exercise, respond, seek God, grow, and change? How long did it last, if it worked at all? Those lists don't work very long for *anyone*, and so we fall back into self-contempt. The problem does not lie with our lack of discipline. The problem is in the approach.

When we have a change of heart on the inside, it manifests itself on the outside, not the other way around. God invites us to join him in the process through which he heals our inner world so he can transform our outer world.

The voice of shame says, *I hate me; I need to get rid of me.* The voice of discipline says, *I've got to fix me because me is not good.* God says, *I love you; let me restore you.* I like that one best.

Jesus, as hard as I try, I can't change myself. Thank you that you don't ask me to. You ask me to turn to you. Restore me! Heal me! Help me know your love more fully so that I might love others and myself with that love. In Jesus's name.

12

---

what God has promised

In this world you will have trouble. But take heart! I have overcome the world.

—John 16:33

Believing you are a beautiful, beloved child of God can feel risky. To risk anything requires that we possess courage. Some versions translate Jesus's command to "take heart" in John 16 as "be of good courage." *Courage* is from the French word *coeur*, meaning "heart." Take heart. Have courage. "Because of me," Jesus said, "you can do this."

Jesus knows that embracing our identity in him and becoming free to be ourselves takes courage! There is a reason we shrink back from love, from our dreams, from our vulnerability. But, friend, the days of shrinking back need to end. With mercy in his eyes, God calls us to be women of courage and confidence.

Confidence is from the Latin words *con* and *fide*, which mean "with faith." Living a life of courage is not about striving to become something or someone else. It is resting by faith in the God who says, "I have called you, and I will do it!" (see 1 Thess. 5:24). Our confidence rests not in us but in the strength and goodness of God.

I am becoming more and more courageous in believing that I am completely loved in this moment and that God isn't waiting for me to get my act together in order to become worthy of his affection. I have only and ever been lovely to God, and so have you. In the steady face of his love, I am changing.

We cannot heal ourselves or free ourselves or save ourselves. We cannot become ourselves all by ourselves. But we are not by ourselves. We are seen and known and strengthened and urged on to the life we were created for by the King of Love. He wants to help us change and grow. We can't do it, but *he can*. He's very, very good at it. It is, in fact, what he has promised to do.

I choose to believe today that God's presence in me is changing me! I can't change myself, but he can and will help me change and grow.

13

---

looking back

*And we know that in all things God works
for the good of those who love him, who have
been called according to his purpose.*

—Romans 8:28

You were born into a story. Your life is a story! It's the story of how your heart has been handled and what you have come to believe about yourself as a result. Do you know your story? You need to. You need to remember. So do I.

Forgetting my life—my mistakes, my victories, my challenges, my sorrows, my *story*—prevents me from moving forward and growing into the woman I am supposed to be. I must remember. I invite you to join me in remembering. It may seem strange that at certain points on our journey we need to look back in order to move forward, but it's true.

The temptation is to look back with regret rather than with mercy. But God's eyes see clearly, and they are filled with mercy. We can be merciful too.

It's not that I remember everything clearly. It comes to me unbidden, my childhood. It is a hint of eternity on the wind, a connection to seasons past, the memory of wonder, of longing, of knowing. I am still three and seven and sixteen. Every day of my childhood shaped who I am today.

My childhood was not idyllic. Since no one's was, I'm guessing it's a pretty safe bet your life hasn't been perfect either. But a deeper understanding of our stories leads to a deeper understanding of ourselves—who we are and who God has made us to be. Yes, there is sorrow there, but there is glory too.

God was there in the difficult moments of your childhood. Calling. Providing. Shielding. Aching. Loving. Why did he allow certain things to happen? I don't know. We won't know until we get to ask him face-to-face. But we do know that he is good and he is for us. One day we will understand completely. For this moment, though, we are being invited to see with his eyes of mercy and learn how he can use our past to craft a beautiful future.

God, show me how you saw me when I was a little girl. What were your thoughts toward me? What words would you use to describe who I was then?

14

---

desperate for God

As a deer pants for flowing streams, so
pants my soul for you, O God.
—Psalm 42:1 ESV

Each one of us has a place in our life where we are not living in the victory we long for. Our struggle might be rooted in our past, in a fear of relationships, or in a need to control our world. That broken place changes how we view ourselves—and makes us desperate for God.

We all have something that brings us to our knees. It isn't something we would ever choose for ourselves or wish on anyone else, but we all have an area—or ten!—in our lives that drives us to need God. We can't free ourselves. We are weak, aware that something inside is broken and starving. It is a wonderful grace when we finally give up and fall down before the One who is strong.

And, my friend, it is not a bad thing that you desperately need Jesus. For some reason, we feel embarrassed by our desperation; we see desperation as a sign that something is terribly wrong with us. Oh no. We were created to desperately need Jesus. We have always needed him, and we always will. I do not believe God caused the pain of our lives, but I do know he uses it to drive us to him.

Father, I believe you work all things together for my good, even the hard things. I ask you to use the areas I am struggling in today to draw my heart closer to yours. I need you more than I need victory in every area. Reveal your love to me today, Father, here in my weakness. You be my strength. I look to you. In Jesus's name.

15

---

the stories that shape us

*But me he caught—reached all the way
from sky to sea; he pulled me out
of that ocean of hate, that enemy chaos,
the void in which I was drowning.
They hit me when I was down,
but GOD stuck by me.
He stood me up on a wide-open field;
I stood there saved—surprised to be loved!*

—Psalm 18:16–19 MSG

As you think about your childhood, do you sense that God is calling you to forgive someone who hurt you? Forgiveness, like repentance, is an act of our will. It is also a commandment from our God. When we forgive others, we are not saying that what they did was all right. No. We are saying that we will not hold on to our pain, our rage, or our sense of injustice any longer. We release those who hurt us to God to deal with, and we refuse to let them hurt us any longer. I choose to forgive my mother. I forgive my father. I even forgive myself. Again.

The painful stories from our past and the words spoken to us that crippled us do not stand a chance in the light of the powerful grace and mercy that come to us now in the person of Jesus. The holy work of God deep in our hearts as we have suffered and struggled and wept and longed to overcome is stunning beyond measure. You may not see the goodness yet, but you will. You will. It comes when we see our lives through God's eyes.

Jesus is inviting us to recover those parts of ourselves that we have tried to hide or lop off in hopes of being more acceptable. God wants us to love him with all our hearts, including the portions of our personalities we would like to change, the dreams long buried, and the wounds we have ignored.

God has not abandoned us, and he never will. Yes, the pain of life is sometimes too intense to bear. But when from that place we cry out to Jesus to save us, the heavens rejoice, the demons tremble in defeat, and the Holy Spirit, who is closer than our skin, transforms us.

Though my past has shaped me, I am not my past. Though my failures and the failures of others have had an effect on who I am, they do not define me. Jesus has won my victory!

16

---

created in the image of God

So God created man in his own image, in the image of
God he created him; male and female he created them.

—Genesis 1:27 ESV

Most little girls at some point dream of living in a fairy tale.
The big surprise when we grow up is not that the fairy tale was
a myth but that it is far more dangerous than we thought.
We do live in a fairy tale, but it often seems as if both the
dragon and the wicked witch are winning. Things are not
what they were meant to be. Fire and ice. Beauty and terror.
Pain and healing. We came into this life gasping for air, and
we are gasping still.

One of the great darknesses of the world is misogyny—the hatred of women. We see stories of violence,
prejudice, and neglect from every country, including our

own. We experience misogyny ourselves in both dramatic and subtle ways.

When Jesus came onto the scene, he turned misogyny on its head. A rabbi at that time wouldn't speak to a woman in public, not even his own wife (this is still true for orthodox rabbis). Even today, an orthodox Jewish man is forbidden to touch or be touched by any woman who is not his wife or a close family relation. Jesus didn't abide by those rules. During his ministry Jesus engaged with women many times. He spoke to them. He touched them. He taught them. He esteemed them. He allowed women to minister to him physically, touching him, washing his feet, anointing him with oil and with their tears. Women disciples traveled with him, supported him, learned from him, and sat at his feet. If the church, the body of Christ, had followed the example Jesus set instead of the traditions of men held captive to sin and the fall, we would have a much higher history here.

The good news is that Life has won out. Yes, we remain in the battlefield, in the middle of a world that often demeans and hurts women. But God loves women. Jesus loves women. And as we become more ourselves, we come to love who we are as women and recognize all we have to offer a broken world.

Jesus, thank you for your love for women in a world that does not always love us. Even in the midst of this battle, help me live with love, not bitterness. Bless my femininity and help me bless it so that I might know you more! In Jesus's name, amen.

17

more than conquerors

*For our struggle is not against flesh and blood, but
against the rulers, against the authorities, against
the powers of this dark world and against the
spiritual forces of evil in the heavenly realms.*

—Ephesians 6:12

The source of evil against women and girls in this world is not men, not the church, not even governments or systems of injustice. Scripture makes it clear that the source of evil is the Evil One himself. If we blame anything else, nothing will change.

Jesus called Satan the prince of this world. Satan is the prince of darkness, whose sole aim is to steal, kill, and destroy life in all its forms. He has power here on earth, wherever the kingdom of God is not being enforced or advanced. He is the source of the hatred of women and girls, the hatred you have endured. But let us remember: Jesus has won all victory through his crucifixion, resurrection, and ascension. All authority in heaven and on earth was given back to him, where it rightly belongs. And then Jesus gave it to us.

When we come to understand that Satan is the cause of hatred against women, we can not only make leaps forward in understanding our lives but also find our way through the battle to the goodness God has for us and the goodness he wants to bring through us.

There is a reason the Enemy fears women and has poured his hatred onto our very existence. Let him be afraid, then. We are more than conquerors through Christ who strengthens us, and we will not be overcome. God is our strength. Jesus is our defender. The Holy Spirit is our portion. And in the name of our God and Savior, we will choose to love him. We will choose to bow down in surrendered worship to our God. And by the power of Christ in us, we will choose to rise up and be women of God, bringing his kingdom in unyielding and merciful strength.

God, thank you for creating women and girls with a unique and vital role in this world. How are you calling me to use my gifts and power as a young woman today?

18

coheirs with Christ

We are hard pressed on every side, but not crushed;
perplexed, but not in despair; persecuted, but not
abandoned; struck down, but not destroyed.

—2 Corinthians 4:8–9

Just as we cannot overcome our feminine bodies by hating them, we cannot overcome misogyny by hating girls. When we hate other girls, we hate ourselves. When we diminish the role of women in the world, we diminish ourselves. When we are jealous or envious, slandering other girls, we join the Enemy's assault on them. In doing those things we come into agreement with the Enemy of our hearts and of God by saying that what God has made is *not* good.

It's time to stop doing that. The way to navigate the battle begins with love. Not blame, not finger pointing, but love.

Let us begin by celebrating the role we play. Let us champion these callings and celebrate them every way we can. The truth is that who we are as women, what we bring, and the role we play in the world, in the kingdom of God, and in the lives of men, women, and children are of immeasurable worth and power.

The kingdom of God will not advance as it needs to without women rising up and playing their role. The transformation and healing of a man requires the presence, strength, and mercy of a woman. Men will not become the men they are meant to be without godly women pouring into their lives. Women will not become who they are meant to be without the strength, encouragement, and wisdom of other women nurturing their lives.

You, as a young woman, are an image bearer of God. You are a coheir with Christ. You are valued, worthy, and powerful. Your valiant feminine heart is needed today in the lives of those you live with, go to school with, and love.

Father God, I repent of the ways I cut down other young women, judge them, gossip about them, or nurture feelings of envy and jealousy. I thank you for my life, and I choose life. I give my life fully to you now, Jesus, and I invite you to have your way in me. I pray all of this in your glorious and beautiful name, Jesus Christ. Amen.

19

beautiful girl

As a mother comforts her child,
so will I comfort you.
—Isaiah 66:13

The things we learned or that were passed on to us from our mothers shape us. Maybe what was passed on to you wasn't so great, but it does not have the final say on who you will become. Jesus has come for you! You have been adopted into a new family, and you have a new bloodline.

Mothers have the ability to withhold acceptance, value, love. Our mothers failed us when, without meaning to, they passed on to us low self-esteem. Or based our self-worth on anything other than the fact that we exist.

God does not do that. Our worth is not based on what we do, which life path we choose, or what we believe. Our worth is inherent in the fact that we are image bearers of the living God.

If we were not of great worth, then the blood of goats and lambs, oxen and bulls would have been enough to purchase humanity out of captivity. Back in the garden of Eden, you remember, the human race went into captivity, and the price to buy us back was so high that no ransom note was even sent. But God knew and pursued us. He intervened.

Let God continue to mother you, to heal you. Continue to pray and press in toward the more that God has for you. And know that, whether she conveys it to you or not, you are a *gift* to your mother's heart. Every mother learns more from her children than she ever teaches them.

You were a beautiful little girl who was deeply loved, a beautiful little girl who had a heavenly Father who delighted in her, grieved with her, and worked in her life even in unseen ways. You are of immeasurable value. You have a worth beyond counting.

How has your mother's view of herself, her body, and her role as a woman affected your view of yourself? Invite Jesus in to reveal how he sees you. Pray a blessing over your mother that she, too, can increasingly see herself as God sees her!

20

---

a quiet soul

But I have calmed and quieted my soul,
like a weaned child with its mother;
like a weaned child is my soul within me.

—Psalm 131:2 ESV

No one has a perfect mother. You don't. I didn't. Your mom didn't. My sons didn't. A perfect mother does not exist. We have all been failed by our mothers to one degree or another. We all need healing in the places where we were missed or hurt. We need to forgive our mothers for the ways they failed us. We all need God to mother us in the places that need tending.

This is where the beauty of the mother heart of God comes in. God can meet our every need, heal our every wound, and bring his mercy to the places in our hearts that so desperately need it.

I love Psalm 131. I take it as a promise that regardless of what we do or do not receive from our mothers, there is hope for us. There is healing. Nothing is out of reach for Jesus. *Weaned* means satisfied. *I am satisfied. I have had enough. All is well.* A weaned child is a satisfied child. Full. Content. We can know that. In the deepest recesses of our hearts, we can know that. Dear ones, we *can* be satisfied. God put us in a world where we have him and we have one another.

A woman once told me that there are all kinds of ways God brings daughters into our lives, and I have found that to be true. Well, it is also true that there are all kinds of ways God brings us mothers too. Spiritual mothers. Friends. Counselors. Christ himself.

If you don't have women who are mothering you these days, ask God to bring them. And, as always, let God continue to mother you, to heal you. To guide, instruct, and comfort you. He's very good at it.

Jesus, I have hope that you can satisfy me. Even though I have pain from my childhood and pain in some of my family relationships today, I believe that in you I can be content. My soul is quiet before you now. Amen.

21

the only reflection that matters

Has anyone by fussing in front of the mirror ever gotten taller by so much as an inch? All this time and money wasted on fashion—do you think it makes that much difference? Instead of looking at the fashions, walk out into the fields and look at the wildflowers. They never primp or shop, but have you ever seen color and design quite like it? The ten best-dressed men and women in the country look shabby alongside them.

—Matthew 6:27–29 MSG

My mother used to say, "Beauty before pain!"—meaning, being beautiful is more important than not feeling terrible. High heels with our toes pinched into the pointy tip. Spanx. Waxing. Trimming. Plucking. Paying!

Maybe that's why I spend far too much time in front of a well-lit magnifying mirror, criticizing my skin, my face, and those horrible chin hairs that seem to come from nowhere. My husband encourages me to throw out that mirror. Maybe I'll be ready when I've attained a hair-free status. Or better, maybe I'll throw it away when my soul more fully embraces the truth of what God says about me.

The truth is, God has been inviting me to throw the magnifying mirror away for years. He has been inviting me to be free from gazing at the multiple imperfections in my face and in my soul and instead to believe the reflection he is showing me.

The only reflection that really matters is the reflection we see in God's loving and joyous eyes. What does he see? What does he say? He says we are beautiful *now*.

How do you see me today, Jesus? When you look at me closely, when you study me, what do you see? Help me see myself as you do.

22

measuring up

O LORD, you have examined my heart
and know everything about me.
—Psalm 139:1 NLT

Theodore Roosevelt said, "Comparison is the thief of joy."
He's right. It's so easy in this world to compare ourselves to
others. When we do that, we simply do not measure up. We
tend to compare our worst with another person's best, and
that makes us feel terrible. Feeling despair over who we are
or what we look like causes us to reject ourselves.

And that is the opposite of what Christ does.

He says you are just right, right now. His invitation
to you in this very moment is to accept your body, your
personality, all of yourself. Just as you are. He made you
you. He's not waiting for you to become something other
than who you are in order to be loved by him. He loves you

now. He accepts you now. He not only accepts you but he embraces you, and he wants you to embrace yourself as well.

Now, I know that embracing ourselves is a stretch for most of us, but please know that embracing ourselves has nothing to do with arrogance or settling for a lower version of who we are. Embracing ourselves has everything to do with embracing the goodness of God's creative work in us. It means trusting God, believing that all he has made is glorious and good. And that includes you. You are the only one who can be you. The world, the kingdom of God, and all those around you need you to embrace who you were created to be as you become more fully your true self.

If you could do anything at all and know it would go really well, what would you do?

23

God's gift

He brought me to the banqueting house,
and his banner over me was love.

—Song of Solomon 2:4 KJV

Our bodies are God's gift to us through which we experience the world. Our five senses are windows that illuminate our lives. Just as we need to be kind to our hearts, we need to be kind to our bodies. We need to pay attention to when we are hungry and feed our bodies nourishing food. We need to notice when we are tired, not ignore the signals, and give ourselves rest. We want to strengthen our bodies with exercise and movement. We want to say nice things to ourselves about our bodies.

Does that last sentence sound strange to you?

Just last night, I caught myself telling myself that my body is ugly. I repented. I said out loud, "No. My body is not ugly. I love my body. I am beautiful."

That's how it works. I caught myself being mean, so I stopped. I chose instead to say to myself what God says about me, and honestly, it had a powerful, life-bringing effect.

The season of growth you find yourself in may make you uncomfortable with how your body is or isn't changing. We grow. We lose weight. We gain weight. Our hormones go nuts. Our breasts get larger … or they don't. (The truth is, most women I know are now or have been ashamed by or disappointed with their breasts. I have been.)

But shame and embarrassment over your body does not have to be part of your story at any age. There's no shame in Christ, friends. No shame.

Speak words of truth to yourself right now: "I am pretty." "I am loved." "God says I'm lovely." "God loves my incredible, amazing, beautiful body!" There is power in saying the truth out loud!

24

worth caring for

If you open your eyes wide in wonder and belief, your body fills up with light. If you live squinty-eyed in greed and distrust, your body is a dank cellar. If you pull the blinds on your windows, what a dark life you will have!
—Matthew 6:22–23 MSG

When we look in the mirror, we see the flaws. We see our shortcomings. What is barely noticeable to others is glaringly ugly to us.

In junior high I would hide my face behind my hair. I wore my hair long and straight and tried to have only my nose poke out. That's because my cheeks were covered with pimples. Not little whiteheads but deep, red, large blemishes.

Sweetheart, you are not alone, and this is not the end of your story. The bodily changes of becoming a woman can be hard and painful, but they will pass.

You are you. Unique. Marvelous. Beautiful. Quirky. And imperfect. In Christ, as with all loved ones, you don't need to hide who you are. You actually aren't meant to hide at all.

It can be hard to be happy with how God made you at any particular time, but especially in the teen years. Those who are tall want to be short. Those who are short want to be tall. Those with curly hair long for straight, and those with straight hair want more body to it. We feel we are too flat or too curvy, too little or too big, not enough or too much. And it doesn't feel good.

But you are worth caring for. Body and soul. You are worth accepting. You are worth embracing. How can you care for your body today?

My body, my heart, and my soul are worth caring for today. God created them and they are priceless!

25

God dreams big

For as the sky soars high above earth,
so the way I work surpasses the way you work,
and the way I think is beyond the way you think.
—Isaiah 55:9 MSG

So, who are you? A great way to discover the answer to that is simply to ask, what do you like? What would you do with your life if you were free to do anything at all?

A number of years ago, in a small group I was in, we were invited to dream. We were given paper and told to write down what we wanted. To write a long list. Not to edit it. Nothing was too small or too large to write down. My list turned out to be two pages long and had things on it as varied as the garden I wanted to nurture, the hope to ride horses with my husband, the healing I longed for a few dear ones to experience, and the wedding of a single friend I wanted to dance at.

I found that list a few years ago, and to my astonishment every single item had come true. It had happened!

God dreams big. And he invites us to dream big with him. He has planted dreams and desires in each one of our hearts that are unique to us. Opening up our spirits, our minds, our hearts, our imaginations to what we would really like—to even the possibility of wanting—allows the Holy Spirit to awaken parts of ourselves that are in such a deep sleep that no dreams are happening.

God is a dreamer. He has dreams of you and for you. What dreams might he have for you today?

Jesus, I want to know the dreams you have for me. I want you to shape my dreams and show me what they say about who you are. Amen.

26

what can God not do?

"For I know the plans I have for you," declares
the LORD, "plans to prosper you and not to harm
you, plans to give you hope and a future."
—Jeremiah 29:11

When we dream with God, we don't want to start thinking immediately, *How can I make this happen?* Dreaming with God isn't about *how*. It's about *what*. If anything could happen, then what would I love to see happen in my life? What would I love to see happen in the lives of those I love?

It's much easier to dream for other people, to have desires for our family and friends. We can fairly easily name what we want their lives to look like, the healing and the freedom we'd love for them to come to know. It's a wee bit more difficult to dream for our own lives.

But this book is about *your* heart. This moment is about your dreams and your desires that contribute to the unique, marvelous young woman you are. The point is not so much being able to name the desire as it is to allow God to access the places in our hearts where dreams and desires are planted. God speaks to us there. About himself. About ourselves.

It's okay to want, and it's okay to want *more*. Wanting more has nothing to do with feeling unsatisfied or lacking in your present reality. It's being open to the more that God wants to bring to your life. The possibilities for you are limitless! Yes, they are. Maybe not for tomorrow but for your *life*.

What can God not do? What is too hard for him to accomplish in your relationships, achievements, creativity, and in the fullness of the expression of who you are? We want to be women who continue to grow all our lives. We never want to stop. Yes, we rest. But a heart alive is a heart that is awake and curious and pressing in to more.

Lord, help me dream the dreams you have of me and for me. Today, I let go of how they can happen, and I open my heart and mind to all the possibilities you have for me. In Jesus's name, amen.

---

a heart awake

Abraham never wavered in believing God's promise. In fact,
his faith grew stronger, and in this he brought glory to God.
—Romans 4:20 NLT

According to David Kohl, professor emeritus at Virginia Tech, people who regularly write down their dreams and desires earn nine times as much over their lifetimes as people who don't. (Think of what you could do with that! What good could you bring? What adventures could you have?) Life dreams come true for people who allow themselves to dream, who own their dreams, and who write them down and look at them periodically.

Sixteen percent of Americans say they have dreams but don't write them down. Four percent have dreams and desires and write them down, but less than 1 percent review and update them on a regular basis. But most Americans (80 percent) say they don't have any dreams, and we can imagine why. Life can suck the dreaming right out of you. The living God wants to pour those dreams back in.

I encourage you to risk dreaming and writing your dreams down. Once you get started, you'll find there are things you want. And if you can't get started, another approach is to begin listing the things you like. From the fragrance of lilacs to a cozy blanket in front of a fire to laughing with friends, it's nourishing to become aware of what you enjoy and to write it down.

It's good to sit with God in the quiet and ask him, *What do I want?* and *What do you want for me?* Awakening and owning the dreams God has placed in our hearts isn't about getting stuff or attaining something. It's about embracing who we are and who he has created us to be. He is our dream come true and the one true love of our life. But we can't love him with our whole hearts when our hearts are asleep. To love Jesus means to risk coming awake, to risk wanting and desiring.

Does it feel dangerous to dream? Risky to hope? Consider this: We can't out-give God. We can't out-love him, and we can't out-dream him. Give yourself permission to dream big! Dream deep. Dream wide.

Nothing is impossible with God. Nothing is too good to be true. After all, if you don't have a dream, how can you have a dream come true?

Jesus, come. Guide me. Holy Spirit, fill me. Dream with me and in me. Help me to unlock the desires you have planted in my heart and to write them down. Help me dream big.

28

---

squeezing ourselves into beauty

For everything created by God is good.
—1 Timothy 4:4 ESV

What the world defines as beautiful varies among cultures and changes over time.

"This is what is beautiful," we are told. "Look like this! Try to be this! You never will be able to, but please keep trying because we are making a lot of money out of your continued failed attempts."

It can make you feel horrid. I think it's meant to. I think it's actually wicked.

We are not supposed to measure ourselves by the world's mirror. There is not lasting life there.

While much of the world is suffering for a lack of food, the diet industry is making billions. *Billions.* Programs and products promising weight-loss cures and lean bodies deliver only a taste of hope. They are tastes that don't last because the programs don't work. But we don't know that. We blame ourselves, and our inner agony turns into self-contempt.

We lose hope. Then we hear of something new, and what the heck, let's give that a try. I know. I've tried almost all of them. They don't work because we are trying to squeeze ourselves into beauty from the outside. True beauty, just like true transformation, is an inside-out process. It's internal first. *It's about your heart.*

Of course you want to be beautiful. But the truth is, you already are! So am I. May God help us all to believe it more deeply and more often. In the places where we don't believe it, we continue to shame ourselves. And shame will never lead us into the life we want to live.

A woman becomes truly beautiful when she knows she is loved. Remember, you are made in the image of God! God is nothing if not absolutely gorgeous. Just look at the splendor of creation! The works of an artist tell you something about the person. Look around. God is stunning. And so are you!

Father God, I look around at all you have made and I am in awe! You have put beauty into every piece of your creation, from the mountains to the stars to a blade of glass. I know I am your creation as well—your most beautiful creation. Thank you that you love me above all you have made. Amen.

29

true beauty

Your beauty should not come from outward adornment, such as elaborate hairstyles and the wearing of gold jewelry or fine clothes. Rather, it should be that of your inner self, the unfading beauty of a gentle and quiet spirit, which is of great worth in God's sight.

—1 Peter 3:3–4

What was Peter saying in this passage? He wasn't saying, "Don't fix your hair" or "Don't wear jewelry." He wasn't saying, "Only wear frumpy, out-of-style clothes." No! He was saying, "Don't fixate on your outward appearance, but center your attention on your heart."

Your beauty is under siege. It is being harassed and taunted and mocked because it matters. You matter. The Enemy of your soul attacks the core of your heart by attacking your beauty in order to pin your heart down and keep you from being the young woman you truly are. You are a powerful child of God. Your beauty is powerful. As an image bearer of the living God, you possess a beauty that is deep and true and core to your soul. It manifests itself on the outside but is first and foremost an inward quality. It blooms in the soil of confidence, assurance, and a happy heart. Let me tell you a secret: *you are at your most outwardly beautiful when you aren't obsessing over your outward beauty.*

"A gentle and quiet spirit" does not refer to a woman who barely talks above a whisper and never gets angry. "A gentle and quiet spirit" speaks of a heart that is filled with faith. Not doubt. Not fear. Not anxiety. Faith. Beauty flows from the heart of a young woman who is resting in the truth that she is loved, seen, known, wanted, and lovely to her heavenly Father. Right now. That young woman lives with self-confidence. And self-confidence is beautiful.

You can have that. You are a true beauty. Really. And it is right and good that you want to be, because you are a reflection of Beauty himself.

Jesus, thank you for calling me beautiful. I don't feel sure of it all the time, but I believe you are sure, and I want to open myself to whatever you want to do in me. Thank you for loving me! Amen.

30

Jesus can

Apart from me you can do nothing.
—John 15:5

Do you ever feel like you can't change yourself the way you want to? You're right. You can't. But Jesus can. *Christ in you can.* He is the secret! God is beautiful and God is fearless. Jesus, who died on the cross for you, entered into the worst nightmare imaginable and demanded that Satan hand over the keys to hell. Jesus rose triumphantly and is seated at the right hand of God. This same Jesus

- calmed the storm and walked on the water;
- healed the leper and fed the thousands;
- gave sight to the blind, hearing to the deaf, and life to the dead;

- cleared the temple and received the children; and
- rebuked the Pharisees, forgave sinners, and cast out demons.

And he is still doing it. Jesus is alive today and living his beautiful, bold, glorious life through you. Christ is your life and your breath and your hope and your courage. In him you live and breathe and have your being. And apart from him, you can do nothing. Once you have accepted Jesus as your Lord and Savior, received his death in your place, received his forgiveness for your sins, and invited him to take his rightful place and rule your heart, you will never be apart from Christ again.

You are in the palm of his hand, and nothing can take you out. That's the secret of being truly beautiful! We increasingly lean on Jesus, calling on him to live his life through us. And as he does, we are transformed into the very image of God.

Jesus, the more I get to know you, the more I realize I can do nothing good apart from you! The more I get to know you, the more I realize that only in knowing you can I truly come to know who you created me to be.

31

---

our artist God

He spreads out the northern skies over empty space;
he suspends the earth over nothing.
He wraps up the waters in his clouds,
yet the clouds do not burst under their weight....
And these are but the outer fringe of his works;
how faint the whisper we hear of him!
Who then can understand the thunder of his power?

—Job 26:7–8, 14

Some things can be measured scientifically. Weight. Height. Age. All kinds of things can be measured.

But how do you measure the beauty of a comforting touch? The joy of a smile? The warmth of an embrace? Tears of empathy? Eyes that welcome, accept, and love? How can you quantify the sound of a laugh that makes you feel to your bones that all is right in the world?

How can you possibly dissect beauty? That would be like pinning a dead butterfly to a board. What then would you know of the wonder of its flight or what is drawn from the heart while watching its aerial dance?

Outward beauty is a thing that can be measured only when we accept the standards of measurement. Youth passes, so youthful beauty fades. But who wants to live in a cage, fearful of the ravages of time? Life is to be lived! Beauty, true beauty, increases. It increases over time as it is offered, shared, and spent on others. It increases as our eyes open to the beauty surrounding us in God's creation and in each and every one of his image bearers. It grows as Jesus captures more of our hearts with his own and we are transformed into his very likeness. It expands as we believe we are who he says we are: his very beloved.

How can you measure the beauty of a sunset? Of a child laughing? Of the living God? Of you?

Love is always the highest goal. Love of God, love of others, and love of ourselves. We don't want to live in spite of ourselves, but we want to embrace ourselves, owning the multifaceted, mysterious women we are and the unique way we bring Jesus to the world. God says you are beautiful.

More beautiful than any other thing in all creation. And, well, he ought to know.

God says I am more beautiful than anything else in creation. I choose to believe this truth today!

32

free to be ourselves

God is within her, she will not fall;
God will help her at break of day.

—Psalm 46:5

Jesus invites us to relax into the beauty he has bestowed upon us and cease striving to attain a level of smooth perfection that looks wonderful on a doll or magazine cover but is not attainable in the living, breathing realm of humanity. The more we know Jesus as he really is, the more we love him. The more we love him, the more our lives are transformed and the more beautiful we become.

To continue on the journey of becoming free to be ourselves, free to become even more beautiful, we need him to strengthen us when we are too weak to believe. We need him to breathe his fiery love into the chambers within that are frozen by fear. We need him to hold our hope and tend our hearts and tell us once again who we are. We cannot do this alone.

Thank goodness we are not alone. God is with us to help us see ourselves through his eyes.

Dear Father, I need your mercy right now. This day holds too much for me but not too much for you. I give you my day. I give you my life. I trust you to rise up in me and give me everything I need for what lies before me. Thank you that because of you, I will not fall! In Jesus's name, amen.

33

---

who do you think you are?

The one who is in you is greater than
the one who is in the world.

—1 John 4:4

I remember once when I was at church and in a very low place. I felt hideously ugly. I was telling myself that I looked like Jabba the Hutt. (Not very nice words to say to one-self—there is power in naming things.) Kneeling in prayer, I asked God, *How do you see me?* In my sanctified imagination, I immediately saw a woman kneeling. The sun filtering through the window framed her in a golden beam of light. She was wearing a lovely fitted white satin dress. Her hair was softly yet ornately done up, with seed pearls in it. She was a beautiful bride and clearly held in the gaze of her God.

He saw me then as beautiful. He sees me now as beautiful.

When God looks at his daughter—me, you, any beloved one—he does not view her through the veil of her sin, the shroud of her failures, or the canopy of her past. When God looks at us, he sees us through the blood of Jesus. When God looks at you, he sees the righteousness of Jesus Christ. You are a spotless, pure, stunning bride. Oh, how we need to see ourselves as he does! Both who we are in this moment and the woman he is forming in us.

Who do you think you are? Who are you on the road to becoming? Do you have a vision of who you could become? How does God see you? What is his vision of who you are to become? It's vital that we ask him that question. And then wait for his answer.

Having a vision of who you are becoming informs your present. We live today knowing who we are going to be to-morrow. The key is to *choose to believe* we are who God says we are. And then rest in the knowledge that God is the one responsible for our transformation. We lean into him. We will fail. He will not.

I proclaim today that Christ in me is greater than the one who is in the world. I proclaim that through the power of Christ in me, I will rise up to be a woman of God, helping to bring his kingdom to a world of darkness. Amen!

34

---

agreeing with God

We demolish arguments and every pretension that sets
itself up against the knowledge of God, and we take
captive every thought to make it obedient to Christ.

—2 Corinthians 10:5

Descartes famously wrote, "I think, therefore I am." I would add a fill-in-the-blank in each phrase. I think I am _____, therefore I am _____. I think I am kind, therefore I am kind. I think I am chosen, therefore I am chosen. I think I am becoming more loving, therefore I am becoming more loving. I think I am forever bound to sin, therefore I am forever bound to sin.

What do you think about God? What do you think about yourself? Who are you? What do you think life is about? What do you think is true? What we think informs our reality and has a direct effect on how we live our lives. What we focus on, we move toward. What we look at and esteem molds us in its form. What we think is true plays out in our moment-by-moment existence. What are you thinking?

We can no longer afford to let our thoughts run wild. What we think on *matters*. We have to make it a practice to regularly check in on our hearts, our thoughts. What are we believing? What agreements are we making? Why? When we become aware that our thoughts are not aligned with the Word of God, we repent and elevate our thoughts to agree with God. When we become aware of agreements we are making with the Enemy, such as "Life is hard, and then you die" or "I will never change," we break those agreements. Out loud. Even if it feels true. Especially if it feels true! Then send that ugly thing to Jesus and let his truth take root in your thoughts instead.

Break any agreement you have made that goes against the Word of God with this prayer: *I renounce this lie. I break every agreement I have made with my Enemy. I renounce the*

agreement that [I am overwhelmed; I'll never get free; I hate so-and-so; I am stupid, ugly, fat, depressed—name it and break with it]. *I renounce this in the name of Jesus Christ my Lord. I choose to believe only the truth of what you have said in your Word.*

35

spiritual warfare

Be alert and of sober mind. Your enemy the devil prowls
around like a roaring lion looking for someone to devour.

—1 Peter 5:8

Spiritual warfare is designed to separate you from the love
of God. Its goal is to keep you from living in the freedom
that Jesus has purchased for you. When we have failed or
sinned or are feeling horrid, Satan whispers to us that we
are nothing and no one. He is a liar. And our fight for our
freedom involves exposing him for who he is, even when the
lies feel completely true. The battle is waged and won in our
thought life: in our minds and in our hearts.

So, Spiritual Warfare 101: You have an Enemy. You are
hated. Evil exists. Satan exists. Foul spirits exist. Peter writes
that Satan wants to *devour* us. Devour, not tempt. Devour,
as in shred, maul, kill, destroy. If we do not submit to God,

the Devil will not flee. If we do not resist the Devil, he will not flee. There is no reason to fear or to strive. But we do need to submit to God and resist the Devil. We enforce the freedom Jesus has won for us by believing and agreeing with the truth.

It's time to rise up, girl! Spiritual laws need to be enforced, just like traffic laws. When you are dealing with fallen angels, think about modern-day pirates, sex traffickers, the Mafia, and other lawbreakers who hate authority, rebel against it, and breathe death and destruction. Demons don't stop harassing you if you don't force them to stop harassing you. So do it now, knowing that your victory is already assured!

Jesus, I come under your authority now. I receive all the work you accomplished for me in your death, in your resurrection, and in your ascension. I take my place in your authority now, and in your name, Jesus, I come against every foul spirit that has been harassing me. Amen.

36

---

take that!

By their fruit you will recognize them.

—Matthew 7:16

You can recognize if you are under spiritual attack or dealing with foul spirits by judging the fruit.

Is misunderstanding coming against your friendships? Pray against that. *I bring the cross and blood of Jesus Christ against all misunderstanding and command it bound to his throne—by his authority and in his name.*

Are you feeling fear? Discouragement? Self-hatred? The fruit of all that is pretty obvious—it is foul, dark, and paralyzing. Resist it in the name of Jesus.

I am not being simplistic. I understand that often many other issues are involved: our brokenness, our sin, our history. Sometimes there's a reason we struggle with certain things. That's why James says we should first submit to God, then resist the Devil.

For instance, let's say you keep getting hit hard with a spirit of resentment. Commanding it to leave will not make it go away if you are entertaining resentment in your heart, engaging it in your imagination, and opening the door to it by ruminating on it in your mind.

First you have to repent of resentment toward others, yourself, and God. You must seek the healing of Jesus in the wounds that allow resentment to come. You need to choose to love Christ right here, in this very place. This is how you submit to God. Then you will have the authority to command it to leave because you've withdrawn the welcome mat.

Familiar spirits are often hard to recognize because they are historic things you have struggled with. For me, as for many, depression is a familiar spirit. But I see the fruit it brings to my life—despair, fear, loneliness—and I know it is not from God. I stop giving in to the lie that I have to be depressed because it's just how I am. Then I have the authority to tell Satan to take that depression and go!

I bring the cross and blood of Jesus Christ against every foul spirit of [What has been attacking you? Shame, accusation, judgment, offense, misunderstanding, fear, panic, dread, hopelessness?]. *I bring your blood and cross against these foul spirits. In the name of Jesus Christ and by his authority, I command every foul spirit bound to the throne of Jesus Christ for judgment. I break every agreement I have made with the Enemy, and I renounce them now. I make my agreement with the truth. Father, please send your angels to enforce this command. Thank you, God. Praise you. I worship you, Jesus. Amen.*

37

---

in the name of Jesus

So [Jesus] gave them permission. And the unclean
spirits came out and entered the pigs; and the herd,
numbering about two thousand, rushed down the
steep bank into the sea and drowned in the sea.

—Mark 5:13 ESV

I like to send foul spirits to the throne of Christ for him to decide what to do with them. I don't just want to cast them out of my room or my house so they can go on to whomever they desire next.

A lot of times, if a foul spirit is coming against you, it's coming against others around you as well. Send it to Jesus. Forbid its return.

Let's say you walk into a room and are suddenly hit with a wave of fear. Or perhaps you go to bed at night and *boom*, you start worrying about the future, your friends, your grades. Fear. There's a mighty strong chance this isn't just you. The Enemy may well be present in the form of a spirit of fear. When that happens to me, here is how I pray:

> *I bring the cross and blood of Jesus Christ against all fear, and in the name of Jesus Christ and by his authority I command every spirit of fear to leave me now; I send you bound to the throne of Jesus Christ. Go. Now. In Jesus's name.*

It's good to name the specific spirit you are coming under. It doesn't give it more power. Instead, it's like opening the door into the cellar and letting the light in. It removes the power. You become aware that you aren't overwhelmed or full of fear or shame. You aren't intimidated. You don't want to die. No, that's coming from a foul spirit. Rebuke it in the name of Jesus Christ.

Pray the above prayer out loud, naming the specific spirit (such as a spirit of fear) that you are coming under today.

38

---

stumbling into grace

But when he, the Spirit of truth, comes, he
will guide you into all the truth.

—John 16:13

In order to recognize a lie, we need to know the truth. Experts in counterfeit money don't spend their time studying counterfeits. They study the real currency. In the same way, to engage in the spiritual battle raging around us, we don't shift our focus to lies or to the Devil. We focus on Jesus. We marinate in the truth of who God is and who he says we are. Then, and only then, will we be able to quickly recognize a lie. And though there are some areas of bondage in our lives where truth is not going to be enough to set us completely free, we will never get any freedom at all without it.

Daughter of Zion—daughter of the true King—you rise up and sit enthroned when you take your position in Christ and command the Enemy to leave. The Enemy has already been disarmed by the cross of Jesus Christ. When we engage in spiritual warfare *we are enforcing* what has already been accomplished. That's how you free yourself from the chains around your neck!

God has done everything, won everything, and given us everything we need to live in freedom. We are meant to walk in it, more and more. We won't walk gracefully into it all the time. But by the grace of God, and with his help, we can stumble into it. One thought at a time. One day at a time.

Does what you are thinking today about yourself, others, or your circumstances align with the Word of God?

39

---

far from eden

When tempted, no one should say, "God is tempting me." For God cannot be tempted by evil, nor does he tempt anyone; but each person is tempted when they are dragged away by their own evil desire and enticed. Then, after desire has conceived, it gives birth to sin; and sin, when it is full-grown, gives birth to death.

—James 1:13–15

A terrible flu swept through our area recently. It hit us hard, but it hit a friend of mine harder. As I talked with her one day, she confessed, "I wish I would learn what God is trying to teach me so I could get over this flu."

What was she assuming about God? She was assuming that sickness was from him. That simply isn't true. Our current address is far from Eden. We live in a fallen world with broken people, and we ourselves are not yet all we are meant to be. The flu goes around. Sickness is not a punishment from God. He is not waiting for my friend to grasp some deeper truth about herself or to repent of some hidden sin before he heals her. He is not holding out on her to finally get her act together in order to bless her. He is not a mean God but a loving one, filled with grace and mercy. It is his kindness that draws us to repentance, not his cruelty. God will use painful trials, even the flu, to hone us, but he doesn't cause them.

Some of you have been taught a theology that God causes all things. So you have to swallow hard and believe that God caused you to be sexually abused, God caused your mother to die young, God caused your friend to betray you.

Oh, friends, this is a horrible view of God and a profound *heresy*. James makes it clear that God does not tempt anyone to sin. But people are tempted every day. So, then, things happen every single day that God is *not* causing. God does not make anyone sin, but people sin every day, *and those sins have terrible consequences*. This is not God doing these things. Do you see what an important difference this makes in our understanding of God's thoughts toward us?

Jesus, I am struggling today. I know you have not caused the pain I am in, but I ask you to be with me here in this pain. Help me see what it can teach me about your love for me and your calling on my life. In Jesus's name.

40

---

victory!

Dear friends, do not be surprised at the fiery
ordeal that has come on you to test you, as though
something strange were happening to you.

—1 Peter 4:12

How do you understand your life? Why is it turning out so differently from what you imagined? What do you make of its randomness? The phone rings, and you have no idea what is coming. It could be great news! It could be a friend inviting you to a movie! Maybe you won a car! Or it could be something much different.

No one gets a pain-free life. I know some girls' lives look pretty perfect from a distance, but only from a distance. You get close and you learn the truth. A life without suffering is a fantasy life, and you don't live in a fantasy. No, your life is much more than the stuff of fairy tales.

Really. There are wicked witches in fairy tales. There are dragons. In fairy tales, big bad wolves devour beloved grandmothers, and little girls wander the woods alone and afraid.

In the Bible, Peter tells us not to let pain surprise us. But we are surprised, aren't we? We wonder what we did wrong or if we're wrong about God. What we believe about God is quickly exposed by pain. What's he like, *really*? Is he mean? Is he harsh? Is he mad at us? Does he not care? Does he not see? Did we fall through the cracks of the universe?

The very first thing painful trials try to do is separate us from God. But being separated from God is the worst thing that can happen, much worse than the most excruciating of trials.

Christianity is not a promise to enjoy a life without pain, nor is it a shortcut through it. It is a promise that pain, sorrow, sin—ours and others'—will not swallow us, destroy us, define us, or have the final word. Jesus has won the victory. And in him so have we.

Dear Jesus, help me to believe you today and to put my trust in your victory rather than in my ability to take a detour around pain. I can't. But even in pain, I confess that you are more than enough for me. In your name I pray.

41

---

invite Jesus in

My heart has heard you say, "Come and talk with me."
And my heart responds, "LORD, I am coming."
—Psalm 27:8 NLT

How do you find peace in the midst of difficult, painful circumstances? Let Peace find you. He's right where you are, right smack-dab in the middle of your life.

In the midst of your joy, your busyness, your sorrow, and your suffering, turn your gaze on Jesus. Invite Jesus in. Ask him to prove to you once again that he is who he says he is. He says he is your Strength. Your Shield. Your Rock. Your Hiding Place. Your Refuge. Your Deliverer. Your great Comforter, your faithful Companion, and your ever-present Friend. Jesus says he is the mighty God, the Prince of Peace. You can trust him.

Jesus is the only one who can meet the deepest needs of your heart, and he wants you to know that he loves you so deeply that he's moved heaven and earth to do it. He is the only one who will never leave you, will comfort you intimately, and will love you perfectly every single moment of your life. Invite him in.

Praise you, Jesus. Thank you for all you have accomplished for me. I love you. I worship you. You are the King of Kings and Lord of Lords, and your name is above every other name that can be given in this age or in the age to come. Amen.

beauty from ashes

The Spirit of the Sovereign LORD is on me,
because the LORD has anointed me
to proclaim good news to the poor.
He has sent me to bind up the brokenhearted,
to proclaim freedom for the captives
and release from darkness for the prisoners,
to proclaim the year of the LORD's favor
and the day of vengeance of our God,
to comfort all who mourn,
and provide for those who grieve in Zion—
to bestow on them a crown of beauty
instead of ashes,
the oil of joy
instead of mourning,
and a garment of praise
instead of a spirit of despair.

They will be called oaks of righteousness,
a planting of the LORD
for the display of his splendor.
—Isaiah 61:1–3

There may not be a more beautiful passage in all of Scripture than Isaiah 61. This is where Jesus declared what he came to do. He came to heal the brokenhearted, to set the captive free. He came to restore us in him and to him. He came to comfort those who grieve, to bestow on them a crown of beauty instead of ashes and a garment of praise instead of a spirit of despair. He says that sorrow may last for the night, but joy comes in the morning. It comes with the morning star. It comes with Jesus. Always.

Jesus, heal my broken heart and release me from all darkness. Comfort me in my suffering. Cleanse me from all evil that has gotten in or taken root in the places of my sorrow. Give me a crown of beauty instead of ashes. Make me beautiful here, Lord, in this. Lift my grief and sorrow and give me the oil of your gladness instead of mourning. Give me a garment of praise instead of a spirit of despair.

---

the doorway of suffering

In all their distress he too was distressed.

—Isaiah 63:9

In the midst of suffering, we need to ask Jesus for his interpretation of what we are experiencing. Our interpretation of the events will shape everything that follows. It will shape our emotions, our perspective, and our decisions.

I've learned that when it comes to suffering, you can have understanding or you can have Jesus. If you insist on understanding, you usually lose both.

When suffering enters into your life, the first thing to do is to invite Jesus into it. Pray, *Jesus, catch my heart.* When painful trials come your way, by all means, ask God what's up—ask him to interpret it for you. But whether he provides understanding or not, invite Jesus in. Keep inviting Jesus into the pain. Invite Jesus into the places in your heart that are rising to the surface through the suffering, whether they be painful memories, unbelief, or self-contempt. Pray, *Please come meet me here, Jesus. I need you.*

Suffering may be the door you walk through that draws you to deeper intimacy with Jesus. Suffering can do that, if we let it. And though it would never be the doorway we would choose, it is one we will never regret walking through.

What is a situation for which you need to pray, *Jesus, catch my heart?*

44

acquainted with grief

Never will I leave you;
never will I forsake you.
—Hebrews 13:5

Let suffering play its sanctifying role. Though God doesn't cause all the trials in our lives, he does use them. He does work all things for our good. He will use pain to expose our false beliefs about our hearts and about his heart. He will use it to prick a place in us that has been wounded before, to reveal our brokenness so God can heal it. He will use suffering to reveal Jesus's faithfulness, kindness, and unending love for us.

You see, there is more going on here than meets the eye. There is a battle raging over the human heart. Will we love God and choose to trust the goodness of his heart in the face of the immense brokenness of the world? Will we stand in our belief that God is worthy of our worship and praise in the face of the immense brokenness in our world?

We can know that in our distress God, too, is distressed. Jesus understands heartbreak, betrayal, abandonment, loneliness, sorrow, and pain. He is acquainted with grief. He cares. He cares for you.

In Hebrews 13, God promises that he will never leave us or forsake us. The original Greek is difficult to translate because of the strong emphasis on *never*—it's a triple negative. God wants you to know that you will never, never, never be abandoned by him. Ever. Never ever. He promises to never leave you or forsake you no matter what you've done or what you are suffering. We hold on to that.

God will never *leave me or forsake me. Never, never, never. I hold on to this promise today.*

45

leaning into God

Thank God no matter what happens.
—1 Thessalonians 5:18 MSG

My mother was a very driven woman. She could be controlling and demanding. She failed in many ways. Not in every way, not by a long shot, but she did have her rough edges.

My mother also loved Jesus. When cancer began to ravage her life at the age of seventy-one, a startling transformation began to take place. My mother softened. She became gentler. She loosened her grasp on control. She lost her edge to demand or criticize. She said "I love you" more than she ever had. The beauty that was always there began to come forth in truly amazing ways. Our last four months together were the best months of love and relationship we ever shared.

My mother suffered intensely during the last months of her life. But in those final months, she leaned into God and came to know his love in a way that filled her heart with peace and joy. During that time, my mom was unable to swallow anything, so she received nourishment via a feeding tube. She hoped that when she crossed over from life to Life, Jesus would be waiting for her with a large, cold glass of water.

A few months after my mom died, I came across a note in her precious handwriting. This is what it said: "I had an unexpected diagnosis, and it has been the most awesome, rewarding, and glorious time God has ever given to me. I thank God the Father, Son, and Holy Spirit from the depth of my soul."

My mother actually gave thanks in her suffering—not *for* the suffering but for what it did in her life. It opened her up to relationship. It enabled her to offer love and receive love. And though her battle with cancer ended up costing her life, what she gained through the pain she considered "the most awesome, rewarding, and glorious time God has ever given to me."

And she's drinking Living Water now!

Jesus, I want to give thanks in my suffering today. Thank you for being in my suffering with me! May the pain I experience cause me to offer and receive love more abundantly. Amen.

46

the work of suffering

And so we are transfigured much like the Messiah, our
lives gradually becoming brighter and more beautiful
as God enters our lives and we become like him.

—2 Corinthians 3:18 MSG

Our friend Scott sent us a little note on the twenty-eighth anniversary of his fall from a ladder that left him paralyzed from the waist down. Scott and his wife know God in a way few of us do. He simply wrote, "No regrets." The note brought my husband, John, and me to tears.

God didn't give my mom cancer any more than he caused Scott to fall. He didn't cause it. But he will use it. He will use it to reveal to us who he really is in the face of tragedy and anguish. He will use it to reveal to us who we really are. Jesus wants you to know who you are. He wants us to see ourselves as our Father sees us. The most important mirror for us to look in is our reflection in his eyes.

I would like to become a woman who is as desperate for God in my joy as I am in my sorrow. That has not happened yet. Nothing brings my heart to fully run after God like being in a season of grief. It may be grief over the way I have failed my sons or my husband. It may be sorrow over a revelation of how my selfishness has hurt my friends. It may be pain over the suffering that one I love is experiencing. But nothing causes me to seek God like pain. Our loving God uses the pain and sorrow in our lives to transform us, again and again.

Dear God, whether I experience joy or pain today, may it draw me closer to you.

47

---

giving thanks

Be exalted, O God, above the heavens;
let your glory be over all the earth.

—Psalm 57:11

How do we allow suffering to do a holy work in us and not let it make us envious, hard, angry women?

We need to be honest about what we *have* done with our suffering. Have we become more fearful? Controlling? Has resentment toward God or others entered in? Let us quickly bring that to Jesus, for this is cancer of the soul, and it ravages what God means to make lovely. Let us renounce our anger or envy, our controlling tendencies or bitterness. Let us ask God to remove these things from our heart and soul.

Nothing—nothing—undoes the harmful effects of suffering as does our choice to worship Jesus in the midst of it. That doesn't mean we must give thanks to God *for* every wicked, evil, hard, painful, excruciating, grief-filled thing that happens in our lives. That would be calling evil good. No, my sister, what the scripture says is to give thanks to God *in* every situation, not *for* every situation.

By loving Jesus in our pain, we allow him *into* our pain. Being thankful opens up windows in the spiritual realm for the presence of God to fill our lives, our thoughts, our understanding, and our perspective. It opens up doors to the blessings God wants to pour into our lives. We will come to a place of increasing gratefulness for the story of our lives, both the joyful times and the excruciating seasons. We are on our way to the place of being able to exalt God over all of it. Yes, all of it.

Father God, use the pain in my life today to reveal your faithfulness, kindness, and love for me! Amen.

48

beautiful scars

Put your finger here; see my hands. Reach out your hand
and put it into my side. Stop doubting and believe.

—John 20:27

When Jesus rose from the dead and appeared to his disciples, Thomas was not present. So Jesus came back to them again, when Thomas was also in their midst. Do you recall how Jesus proved he was real, risen, and still the same Jesus they had always known and loved? He told Thomas, "Put your hands in my scars." Jesus still had his scars then, and he still has them today. They are Jesus's glory. They are what we most worship him for. Glorified Jesus still has his scars, and when we reach glory, so will we. But they will be beautiful, like his.

The story of my life and the struggles I have lived with— and continue to live with—have helped shape me into the woman I am today and the woman I am becoming. My scars, my struggles, my failures, my joys, my private lonely agonies have been forging my soul into something beautiful. Eternal. Good. Yours have too.

Now, we can fight that process—or we can yield to it. We can choose to let suffering soften us or harden us. We can choose whether we will allow it to make us more compassionate or let our hearts become jealous of others. We can choose whether we will love Jesus in it or resent him for it. Only one set of choices will make us more beautiful.

The pain we experience, the sorrow and the agony, serve a purpose. God *is* working all things together for our good. He is etching a masterpiece of stunning design. The beauty being forged in us through the transforming work of suffering is one that will leave us breathless, stunned, and forever thankful. And the crowning glory will be that because of the pain we have endured, we have come to know Jesus in a way that causes us to treasure the trial as one of God's greatest gifts to us. Amazing.

I choose today to let my suffering soften me to God's love. I choose to let my suffering make me more compassionate toward others. I choose to let my suffering make me more beautiful.

49

shake off your dust

Shake off your dust;
rise up, sit enthroned, Jerusalem.
Free yourself from the chains on your neck,
Daughter Zion, now a captive.

—Isaiah 52:2

John and I went to the zoo recently. We saw an amazing selection of birds—flamingos, California condors, and two bald eagles—enclosed in a habitat with high nets.

Later that day, we went for a hike in the hills. We stopped at the cry of a hawk and looked up to see three of them soaring, diving so fast, then up, up, up. Chasing each other, then hovering and still—they flew with the aerial gymnastics of angels. They were awesome. They were *free*.

I felt bad for the birds I had just seen in captivity. At the zoo it had been wonderful to see bald eagles up close. How huge they are! But I've seen bald eagles eating fish on the banks of the Snake River. I've seen them looking out over their domain from the protected heights of a stately pine, and I've seen them battling golden eagles over their nests.

Freedom is better than captivity. So why does anyone choose captivity? Why do we live so long in the bondage we find ourselves in—the bondage of peer pressure, negative thoughts about ourselves, and fear?

I'd like every young woman to hear Isaiah 52: "Free yourself from the chains on your neck." *Free yourself?* Isn't it Jesus who sets us free? Indeed he does. But we have a part to play in our freedom. God calls us to rise up, shake the dust off, sit enthroned.

After a while, those animals in the zoo forget they were made for the open skies, the wild savannas. We don't want that to happen to us. We want to remember that God calls us to choose his grace, his truth, and our identity in him.

What is one thing you would like to be free of today? Sorrow? Regret? Self-contempt, shame, worry, doubts, addiction? In what ways does that struggle keep you in captivity?

50

---

the fight of faith

Now the Lord is the Spirit, and where the
Spirit of the Lord is, there is freedom.

—2 Corinthians 3:17

The other night I was lying on the floor with worship music playing. But I wasn't lying on the floor worshipping. I was wondering. The day had not been a great one. I was exhausted from travel and too many conversations, and I thought the answer to my physical and emotional state would be found in pizza and chocolate ice cream. I chose to spend the entire day in old patterns of living that have never proven helpful.

Lying on the floor, listening to the music, I asked God, *Do you really love me now? Here? How can you possibly love me in this low place?*

But I knew he did. Jesus died on the cross for all my sins, even the ones I have committed over and over and over again.

There was a battle going on for my freedom that day. And it was raging where it almost always rages: over what I would choose to believe.

Jesus has won our freedom in a spiritual showdown with Satan. But our Enemy still refuses to go down without a fight. He knows he cannot take down Jesus, the Victorious One. But he can still wound his heart by wounding ours. Jesus has won our freedom. But we need to receive it, claim it, and stand in it. That is our good fight of faith: believing God is who he says he is and believing we are who he says we are in the face of evidence surrounding us that screams the opposite.

In order for us to live in freedom and become the women we are to become, we need to receive God's love even in our lowest places.

Jesus, I long to be free. I long to know you and love you more deeply. You are worthy. Please remove everything that separates me from knowing you as you truly are and keeps me from living in the freedom you have purchased for me. In Jesus's mighty name, amen.

51

free to fail

It wasn't so long ago that you were mired in that old stagnant life of sin. You let the world, which doesn't know the first thing about living, tell you how to live. You filled your lungs with polluted unbelief, and then exhaled disobedience. We all did it, all of us doing what we felt like doing, when we felt like doing it, all of us in the same boat. It's a wonder God didn't lose his temper and do away with the whole lot of us. Instead, immense in mercy and with an incredible love, he embraced us. He took our sin-dead lives and made us alive in Christ. He did all this on his own, with no help from us! Then he picked us up and set us down in highest heaven in company with Jesus, our Messiah.

—Ephesians 2:1–6 MSG

Did you know you are free to fail today? Because of Jesus, you can be free from the cages of other people's expectations, demands, yokes, and judgments—including your own.

Perfectionism is a terrible prison. You don't need to live there.

Satan's goal is to keep you from living in the freedom that Jesus has purchased for you. Satan whispers to you when you have failed or sinned or are feeling horrid that you are nothing and no one. He is a liar. And your fight for your freedom involves exposing him for who he is even when the lies feel completely true. The battle is waged and won in your thought life: in your mind and in your heart.

You live under grace, not under judgment. You are loved, forgiven, embraced. Your emotions may waver. Your physical strength and spiritual life have variables. One day you are strong in Christ, believing everything God says, and another day you feel weak, doubtful, questioning.

That's okay. You will never be free from needing God. He alone is perfect, valiant, complete. And in him, so are you. But only *in him*.

Jesus, I confess that I strive to be perfect, when only you are perfect. I confess that I strive to make people like me, when your view of me is all that matters.

---

the greatest freedom of all

It is for freedom that Christ has set us free.
Stand firm, then, and do not let yourselves be
burdened again by a yoke of slavery.

—Galatians 5:1

Once we know that freedom is available to us, why would we ever want to stay in the captivity of negative thought patterns, judgment, or fear?

Well, prisons can be safe and comfortable. They can become a known life, a familiar way. Resignation is safe; dreaming is dangerous. Letting someone else control your life is easier than rising up to deny them that control; the relationship will never be the same. Living under shame can feel far easier than fighting for your own dignity. The known is always more comfortable and less risky than the unknown.

But we are offered the greatest freedom of all: freedom of heart, freedom from sin, a freedom that enables us to live and love as Jesus did.

We can be free from

- bondage,
- sin,
- the fear of man,
- shame,
- regret,
- rage,
- disappointment,
- addiction, and
- fear.

We are no longer captives to sin. We are no longer slaves to the Enemy, to the world, or to our own flesh. We have been released. We are not only free *from*; we are free *to*! We are free to be transformed into the very image of Christ. Free to love in the face of hatred. Free to become the fullest expression of our unique selves. Free to offer to others the beauty that God planted in us when he first dreamed of us.

We are free to

- dream,
- be happy,
- be glorious,
- succeed,
- love,
- live,
- forgive, and
- not be bound by any chains.

We have this freedom because of what Jesus has done for us! We have been ransomed, paid for, saved, and freed to be who we really are and do what we are meant to do.

What would you love to be free to do today? Pursue a dream? Let God take control of a situation? Love with abandon? Worship God? Experience Jesus more deeply?

53

---

fitting in

Don't copy the behavior and customs of this world, but let God transform you into a new person by changing the way you think. Then you will learn to know God's will for you, which is good and pleasing and perfect.

—Romans 12:2 NLT

I was driving last summer with some gals, all of whom are really pretty and slender and smart and have a lot of friends. (So, yeah, intimidating gals.) I risked asking them the question, "Do you feel as if you fit in?"

Looking at their lives from the outside, I expected their answers to be, "Yes. Sure!" None of them said that. All five, after a lengthy pause and with lowered voices, confessed, "No, I don't."

We share the feeling of being odd. Weird. We share a fear that if people really knew us, they would run away as fast as they could! We share the feeling that everyone else has it together and we are barely pulling it off. We share the feeling that we don't fit in.

So I want you to know that if you feel as though you don't fit in, you are not alone! But if we try to fit in by the ways we act and speak, we get into all kinds of trouble. We do things, say things, wear things, and even eat things we don't really like because we want to belong.

You are not meant to live alone. You need a couple of friends to share this life with. Your friends may appear to fit in and have it all together or they may seem as if they don't care if they fit in or not, but they likely feel much the same as you.

Friends can be hard to come by. They can wound and hurt and betray. Certainly they will disappoint sometimes. That comes with the territory of being human. But friends can also bless and enrich and deepen every experience of life with joy—and what a gift to have someone who wants to feel odd with you!

Jesus, I thank you for making me unique, even though sometimes I wish I could fit in more! I pray for friends who will accept me for who I am and also challenge me to become more of the woman you created me to be. In Jesus's name.

standing out

There are "friends" who destroy each other,
but a real friend sticks closer than a brother.
—Proverbs 18:24 NLT

We are image bearers of the living God, and one of the best ways our feminine hearts bear his image is in our desire for relationship. We are relational to our core. Just like God, we have a deep desire and capacity for relationship, and just like God, we want to be chosen and wanted. We want to be pursued by others not for what we can do but for who we are. It's a good desire. And it's one that can get us into trouble if we aren't aware of it.

This might be most obvious when we're teenagers facing peer pressure, but the temptation remains when we're adults. We women often tend to judge our worth based on what we think others think of us. In our inner worlds, we feel alone. And being alone is the first thing God named as "not good" (Gen. 2:18).

You are not meant to live alone. But what does a true friend look like? How do we know who to trust when we're feeling as if we don't fit in anywhere?

A good friend loves you when you are hilarious and when you are hurting. A true friend loves you when you are being kind and when you are PMS-ing all over the place. She may not love what you are doing or the dragon you are manifesting, but she loves you. She knows who the true you is, and even in the midst of your living as an imposter to your very self, a friend calls you up and out. A friend sees who you are meant to be and beckons you to rise to the higher version of yourself. A friend doesn't want you to fit in. She wants you to stand out as the person God created you to be.

Jesus, help me to know what a true friend looks like so I can be that friend to others and recognize who is a true friend to me.

55

---

bff

I no longer call you servants, because a servant does not know his master's business. Instead, I have called you friends.
—John 15:15

For many years, I thought that a cherished best, *best* friend would be a woman who understood me at all times and enjoyed *all* the same things I enjoyed. She'd want to go to a movie when I wanted to go to a movie, and she would want to see the same show I wanted to see. She would be passionately in love with Jesus and desire him above all else, and she would always point my heart back to him. I would do the same for her, and she would think I was amazing and wise and justified in my mood swings. She would be available to me whenever I called and would be encouraging and empathetic. She would always get my jokes and want to eat at the same restaurant I wanted to eat at, and she would never be offended by a failure of mine.

Embarrassing, right?

The truth is, I have more than my share of amazing friends. And I am learning that each of these variously gifted women offers something of unique value that the others don't. Their very differences from each other and from me enrich my life! God is meeting my need for friendship, just not through one woman. Some women are blessed with a best friend, but most women aren't. Most of us have a few friends who provide something we need, and we provide something they need. Our hearts are met in many ways by the beautiful offerings of a few. I don't think a human being is actually able to bear the burden of being someone's one and only. God alone can be our One and Only.

God understands us all the time. He is available every moment. People don't and aren't. They have lives and schedules and a myriad of people pulling on them, and that makes them normal and not at our beck and call. Jesus calls us "friend." Oh, to know him more deeply as that. I want to know him as my King and my God and my Friend who

enjoys me fully, accepts me completely, and loves me uncon-
ditionally. Because that is who he is.

*God, you created the universe and yet you call me "friend." I
want to know you more deeply as my best friend, the friend who
is always there for me, always understands me, and always loves
me completely.*

56

---

surrendering

For everything there is a season, and a time
for every matter under heaven.
—Ecclesiastes 3:1 ESV

It was a revelation to me to realize that not every friend in our lives is meant to walk with us through the remainder of our lives. Friendships do change. People change. You change. You are supposed to.

Several years ago I realized I was holding a particular friendship not with a loose hand but with a clenched fist. We had been friends for many years, and I assumed we would be friends for the rest of our lives. I ignored the tell-tale signs of change. This friend had been moving away from me for quite a long while, but I absolutely refused to see it. I wanted what *I* wanted. I thought she was fabulous. Surely she must feel the same way about me!

Somewhere along the way, my desire for relationship turned into demand, and demand is one of the death knells of a friendship. I needed to unclench my fist and in love let my friend go. I also needed to invite Jesus into the places of my heart that had refused to see that it was time to let her go.

Insisting. Demanding. Refusing. These are not actions that lead to the life Jesus has for us.

Releasing. Surrendering. Embracing freedom. These are the actions Jesus calls us to. These are the signs of a loving friendship—a friendship that sometimes needs to let go.

Dear Jesus, are there people I am clinging to in unhealthy ways? Are there parts of relationships I need to let go? I know that apart from you, I can do nothing. How are you leading me to cling to you?

our biggest cheerleaders

As iron sharpens iron,
so one person sharpens another.
—Proverbs 27:17

How well I remember sobbing in the arms of a precious friend when my young family was moving across the country. It felt as if my heart were being torn out.

It can be excruciating to let a friend go or, worse, to be let go of.

How difficult it is when a friendship ends because of offenses, misunderstandings, anger, or betrayal. How searingly painful it is when God calls you to walk away from a cherished friend when love and unity have left the relationship.

Sometimes a friendship ends simply because your paths no longer cross. You change schools. You graduate. A job or a parent's job takes you to a different city. The natural and easy ways that we as friends connect shift under our feet, and it takes enormous effort on *both* sides for the friendship to shift and continue as well. Perhaps it is meant to continue. Perhaps it isn't. Some friends we are called to fight for, and some we are called to release.

We are meant to grow and change and become throughout the duration of our lives, and we need to be surrounded by people who celebrate the person we are becoming. Our true friends are people who are our biggest cheerleaders and encourage us on to the next higher version of ourselves that God is calling us to.

Thank you, God, for people who encourage me to be faithful to you.

58

---

jealousy and envy

A heart at peace gives life to the body,
but envy rots the bones.

—Proverbs 14:30

Walking with a friend through trials requires much tenderness, grace, and wisdom on our part, but it is actually more difficult to walk with a friend through a season of success and blessing: "She was voted Most Popular. No one even notices me." "I wish I had been given the scholarship." "I love her new clothes. I wish I had new clothes."

Be careful! Jealousy and envy are two death knells to a friendship. God does not want us to be jealous of what our friends receive or achieve. We are called to rejoice with them. We want only the best for our friends always.

I know that's a challenge—it certainly is in my own life. Loving people through travail and success requires much from us. God is always at work, sifting and shaping, purifying and clarifying what is in our hearts. To stay in relationship with another person requires first that we stay in relationship with God. He is the only way we can navigate through jealousies that rear their ugly heads or offenses from others that prick our vulnerable hearts.

The truth is, a good part of our becoming takes place in the sanctifying work of relationships. And not because friendship is always a greenhouse either. Trees grow strong because of winds; drought forces their roots to go deeper. There isn't anything on earth like relationships to make you holy. When our frail humanity is revealed in some way we and others don't like, we bring it to God. We ask for forgiveness. We ask for his life to fill us and his love to flow through us, which means "Christ in me, love through me" becomes a regular prayer. It always comes back to Jesus.

Jesus, this is tough for me. I want to choose friends wisely, and I want to stick with those friendships and grow through any hard times. Will you please help me be the kind of friend you want me to be? In Jesus's name, amen.

59

---

let it go

[Love] keeps no record of wrongs.
—1 Corinthians 13:5

Too often we keep lists of wrongs done to us in friendship. We say we forgive—and we may even believe we have—but when offenses come up again, we notice them with a sort of sick satisfaction: "See what I mean?"

The word used in Scripture for *offense* actually means "bait," like the bait that is placed inside a trap to lure an animal to its death. When we dwell on our hurts, we have taken the bait of offense. We are inside the trap.

Unless offenses are forgiven, they will poison the relationship. The poison seeps out and affects our own souls as well. Offenses we hold on to lead to death.

Jesus took all our offenses into his broken body when he died for us, and he took everyone else's as well. All that he suffered—the beating, the scourging, the mocking, and finally the crucifixion—was more than enough to pay for it all: our offenses and theirs.

With the help of God, we must choose to forgive. Let it go. Let them go. Come out of the trap.

Dear God, I forgive all those who have hurt me, and I bless them in Jesus's name. I pray only more of you to them, for them. And I forgive myself for having hurt others. Please fill me with your Spirit and live and love through me that I might become a woman after your heart who loves others well. In Jesus's name, amen.

60

---

the power of words

The tongue has the power of life and death.

—Proverbs 18:21

There's a reason there's a movie with the title *Mean Girls*. It's because girls can be vicious. They can bully—in person and on social media. They can gossip. They can ignore, snub, and tell lies.

The saying "Sticks and stones may break my bones but words will never hurt me" is a flagrant lie. Words wound. We are female. We use words. So does God. He *is* the Word. We are meant to follow his lead and use our words to bless and encourage and bring life.

The great thing is, we can do that! How exciting to think that we can partner with the Holy Spirit in creating little islands of hope and kindness and faithful friends amid the sea of unkindness that too many girls experience.

Jesus, I live in a world where cruel words, untrue words, and wounding words are spoken every day. Help me use words to bring light, truth, and healing instead. I want to partner with you to use powerful words in good ways. Amen.

honestly

*We will speak the truth in love, growing in
every way more and more like Christ.*

—Ephesians 4:15 NLT

Scripture exhorts us to speak the truth *in love*, which means
we shouldn't speak the truth in anger or resentment or with
the desire to wound. We need to be careful to check our
underlying motives for speaking the truth. We should be
aware of the reason behind our desire to share something.
We want to know we are speaking the truth with the desire
to love and to bless.

And the Bible does *not* exhort us to speak everything
that is true. In our culture of honesty, we may feel compelled
to share everything with our close friends, even the negative things. We want to be honest, right? We don't want to
have secrets from each other, right? Wrong. Sharing every

thought or emotion that goes through your head will wreak havoc on the relationship.

No friendship has the capacity to carry the burdens of our every nuance. Only Jesus does. He knows us. We don't shock him. We are not too much for him. Sharing truth with a friend in the desire to keep nothing between you can overwhelm the person and the relationship. No relationship can sustain the brunt of total honesty. Relationships are not meant to be the dumping grounds of every negative thought, belief, or emotion.

Yes, confession is good for the soul, but confession to whom? And good for whose soul? It is not good for the person you had hurtful thoughts about! Wounds can be healed. Damage can be addressed. Forgiveness can be bestowed. But words cannot be erased. We can do great damage to one another in the name of honesty.

As we grow into the fullness of who God created us to be, we speak only the truth that God calls us to speak, in love, and only when he calls us to speak it.

Jesus, you are my best friend. You are someone I can be completely honest with, someone who loves me completely. What can you and I do together today to enjoy our friendship? I really want to hear you!

62

unholy bonds

May I never boast except in the cross of our
Lord Jesus Christ, through which the world has
been crucified to me, and I to the world.

—Galatians 6:14

With some people it feels as if they are sucking the life out of you. That is because they *are* sucking the life out of you. There is an ungodly tie there. You need to break it.

When someone worries about you or is angry with you to the point of not being able to feel anything else, judges you, or holds conversations with you when you aren't even present, that is an unholy bond. These types of unhealthy ties create all sorts of havoc. They form a kind of spiritual walkway over which another person's spiritual warfare travels to you. The negative emotions, demonic strongholds, or accusing spirits that have been accosting that person come over and accost you. The soul tie is a two-way street, by the way, so what you are struggling with goes over to her as well.

Galatians 6:14 declares that through the cross of Christ, "the world has been crucified to me, and I to the world." The cross changes every relationship. Even family ties. Jesus tells us, "Anyone who loves their father or mother more than me is not worthy of me; anyone who loves their son or daughter more than me is not worthy of me. Whoever does not take up their cross and follow me is not worthy of me" (Matt. 10:37–38).

All ties are subject now to the rule of Christ. And so we can say, in a very godly and healthy way, "I am crucified to the world, and the world is crucified to me. I am crucified to my mom, to my sister, to my friend, and to my enemy, and they are crucified to me."

The only bond Scripture urges us to maintain is the bond of love by the Holy Spirit. All others—well, it's time to break them. You won't believe how free you can be and how good you can feel!

It is very important to note that breaking a soul tie with a person is not the same thing as *rejecting* the person. It is actually the *loving* thing to do. You don't want the person obsessing about you, and you don't want to be obsessing about her. You don't want her controlling you, and you don't want to be controlling her. You certainly don't want her warfare, and she doesn't want yours.

This simple prayer that follows will help you break unholy bonds.

By the cross of Jesus Christ, I now sever all soul ties with _____ in the name of Jesus Christ. I am crucified to her, and she is crucified to me. I bring the cross of Christ between us, and I bring the love of Christ between us. I send _____'s spirit back to her body, and I forbid her warfare to transfer to me or to my domain. I command my spirit back into the Spirit of Jesus Christ in my body. I release _____ to you, Jesus. I entrust her to you. Bless her, God! In Jesus's name, amen.

63

---

friend me

Be devoted to one another in love. Honor
one another above yourselves.

—Romans 12:10

Social media is here to stay. It has its good points and its dangers. It's a useful way to stay connected and to share life. But it is not a substitute for face-to-face, eye-to-eye connection. You can have hundreds of friends online. You can't maintain that many in the real world. And you need to be grounded in the real world.

Jesus had circles of friendship. You need them too. Maybe there are one to three girls you are really close to, girls you trust with the details of your life—your inner world and your outer one. Next there is a larger circle of, say, ten to fifteen girls you are somewhat current with and love to hang out with, but you wouldn't call them at three in the morning. They're in your youth group, your neighborhood, or your school. Then there is the larger circle of acquaintances: folks you pass in the hall and say hi to; friends in your Spanish class or on your soccer team. That is all well and good and normal. You need all of them.

Friends are gifts to us straight from the heart of God to our own, and no one is better at giving perfect gifts than he is. That's what friends are. They are gems to be treasured. Friends lend each other their clothes, their lecture notes, their courage, their ideas, their faith, and their hope. Ralph Waldo Emerson said, "The only way to have a friend is to be one." So let's be one. Let's pray for them. Let's offer kindness and compassion to them. Let's speak the truth in love. Let's forgive them when they hurt or fail us. Let's offer and invite and be the friend to others that we want them to be to us. And all the while, let's entrust our heart to our Forever Friend, Jesus, who truly loves us at all times.

Jesus, help me to be a real friend to others. Redeem social media in my life. Help me to see how it can bring good to my relationships and how it can hurt them. Guide me in knowing the difference. In Jesus's name, amen.

64

male and female he created them

There are three things that are too amazing for me,
four that I do not understand:
the way of an eagle in the sky,
the way of a snake on a rock,
the way of a ship on the high seas,
and the way of a man with a young woman.

—Proverbs 30:18–19

The first thing the Bible tells us about people is that we are made in the image of God. "In the image of God he created them." The second thing we learn is that we are either male or female. "Male and female he created them" (Gen. 1:27). Gender is at the core of humanity. As a young woman, you are feminine. Guys are masculine. In the deepest part of their souls, not merely in their bodies, guys are *guys*. And guys—though of equal value and dignity to girls—are something quite different from them. But you knew that already.

Guys are different from girls inside and out. From the very beginning. Brain development, brain chemistry, and hormone levels vary by gender while infants are developing in the womb. Guys have hearts like yours with the same deepest longing—to be loved—but their other core questions, their core desires, and their fears take a different form.

Every child enters the world with a question that needs an answer. It is simply this: "Am I loved?" Little girls ask the question (primarily of their father), "Do you delight in me? Am I special? Am I captivating?" Boys ask something else. They need to know they are strong. Their question is more along the lines of, "Do I have what it takes? Am I the real deal?"

Our core questions are different, and so are our core fears. A girl's deepest fear is abandonment. (At some deep level, don't you fear being abandoned and alone? That's because you are made to never be alone. You are relational to your very center.) A guy's deepest fear is failure. Not being strong enough for tough situations.

We are different. Different is good. And we are here on earth to learn how to love. Love God. Love others. Love those like us and those very different from us. And love ourselves too! That's a tough thing to learn and requires a lifetime to do it well. Still, all throughout our lives, we get to grow in learning how to love! We get the honor of partnering with God in loving others. We get to grow in knowing how deeply he loves us each and every day. What a gift!

Dear God, thank you for making guys and girls different, even though the differences and misunderstandings drive me crazy sometimes! Help me to love well, including myself.

65

a safe place

Do not arouse or awaken love
until it so desires.
—Song of Solomon 2:7

Love is good. Love is grand. Sexual attraction is a gift. Actually it's holy ground. You are holy ground. So are boys. So treat them the way you want to be treated and require that you be treated with respect as well.

When a guy smiles at you, it can make your day. When a guy pursues you (if he is the one you like), it can make you so happy. The problem is that rejection from a guy can break your heart. You don't want to give to young men the power to tell you who you are—how valuable, how lovely, or how wanted. They don't have the right to validate you as a woman.

They cannot answer the deepest questions of your heart. Only God your Father can do that. Your soul is meant to live in a place of security. You are to know you are forever surrounded by love every moment of your life. You are wanted. You are beautiful. You are chosen. You are pursued. Jesus has done everything, given everything, and won everything to win you because you are everything to him.

Guys are fabulous, and romantic relationships are thrilling. But even in the best of times, your heart needs to know you are loved and wanted outside and apart from everyone and anything else. Relationships change. God doesn't. His love is the only forever and always safe place for your heart.

Jesus, you know my heart more than anyone. Your love for me never changes. I give you my heart today; take it fully. In Jesus's name, amen.

66

---

boys, boys, boys

Trust in the LORD with all your heart,
and do not lean on your own understanding.
In all your ways acknowledge him,
and he will make straight your paths.
—Proverbs 3:5–6 ESV

I don't think guys are dangerous. I think they're wonderful. Giving your heart away is dangerous. Giving your body away is dangerous. But guys? They're awesome. I love them. (I'm the mother to three fabulous ones.) There are really good ones out there who are strong, kind, noble, deep, handsome, caring, funny, adventurous, creative, brave, and have amazing and good hearts. Even so, they're a grand mystery.

Their souls are deep waters. Their feelings get hurt. They long to be respected. Believed in. Told they are strong. They need the validation of their masculine hearts. And as with yours, it needs to come from their heavenly Father.

Most young men haven't had their questions answered in the way they were meant to. Your heart has been wounded and so have theirs. Just as your heart has been wounded in the core of your femininity, theirs has been wounded in deeply masculine ways. With a heart that has deep, unaddressed questions, it's an easy temptation for a young man to hand over the validation of his life to a girl. When he looks to a young woman to tell him he's got what it takes, he makes as big a mistake as you do when you look to him to tell you you're captivating. But most young men don't know that yet.

Be kind to them. Encourage their strength. Point them to Jesus. Treat their hearts with respect and be mindful of your effect on them. It's greater than you realize.

Jesus, the guys in my life need you as much as I do. They need you to affirm who they are. They need you to help them become who you created them to be. Help me to remember that and help them to know how much you love them. Amen.

67

God's treasure

*I will pray the Father, and he will give you
another Counselor, to be with you for ever.*

—John 14:16 RSV

I read an article recently that said the way you can really
know what someone is like is by observing how he treats
people in the service industry. It's a good litmus test. The
way of love is never rude. Not to friends, siblings, parents,
or waitresses. How we treat others reveals so much about the
quality of our character. How we live when we think no one
is watching reveals the truth about who we really are.

If you are drawn to a guy, there are some litmus tests
you should apply to see if you should move forward in
the relationship. How does he treat others? What kinds of
friends does he have? Do you like them? Are they good guys?
That says a lot about a person. What does he do for others?

Does he offer to help in any way? Or is life all about him? Does he treat others and himself with respect? If not, there is no way he will treat you with respect. Most importantly, is he pursuing a relationship with Jesus?

These are tricky years you are living in, years to invite Jesus into every day. You can't navigate the waters of your heart, your relationships, or your life on your own. You are not meant to. You do not have to. The Holy Spirit is not only your strength and your comforter. He is your very own counselor, sent to you by God because—well, because we all need one. Not every now and again but in every moment of our lives.

You are God's treasure. You are the center of his affection. He loves you deeply. He wants you to know it, live like it, and treat others the same way. Even those boys. And, very likely, one particular boy someday. Ask for his help to do it. Because helping you is what he loves to do.

God, I need your help to understand that I am your treasure! Only when I really understand that can I truly love well.

68

created to love

God blesses those who are merciful,
for they will be shown mercy.

—Matthew 5:7 NLT

We are meant to be loved, to know love, and to love. When we love others, we risk being hurt by them. Getting hurt happens. The only way not to be hurt is … well, there is no way.

In *The Four Loves*, C. S. Lewis wrote,

> To love at all is to be vulnerable. Love anything, and your heart will certainly be wrung and possibly be broken. If you want to make sure of keeping it intact, you must give your heart to no one, not even to an animal. Wrap it carefully round with hobbies

and little luxuries; avoid all entanglements; lock it up safe in the casket or coffin of your selfishness. But in that casket—safe, dark, motionless, airless—it will change. It will not be broken; it will become unbreakable, impenetrable, irredeemable.[1]

Yes, to love is to be vulnerable. We get hurt, misunderstood, wounded, and even betrayed. To keep on being women who love, we will need to be women who grow in wisdom and who continue to forgive. If you've been hurt by young men, God calls you to forgive them. That doesn't mean you stay in relationship with them. It means you forgive them, release them, and invite Jesus to heal you and help you learn.

Dear God, my heart is hurting. I'm hurt so much by what _____ did. But because I love you and you command me to, because you know what's best for me and know I need

1   C. S. Lewis, *The Four Loves* (New York: Harcourt Brace, 1960), 121.

to, because you have forgiven me, I forgive him. I forgive him for _____. I release him to you. I forgive myself for _____. Jesus, wash my wounded heart with your blood. Cleanse me again from every sin and stain and bleeding place. Speak to me here. I need to know your love again. Here. Thank you that your blood on the cross is enough to cleanse me from every sin I've committed and every sin that's been committed against me. You are enough. I love you. And, Jesus, I also sever all soul ties with _____. I bring your cross and your blood between me and _____. I release him to you. In Jesus's name I pray. Amen.

69

---

the greatest commandment

"Teacher, which is the greatest commandment in the Law?"
Jesus replied: "'Love the Lord your God with all your
heart and with all your soul and with all your mind.'"

—Matthew 22:36–37

What is it that Jesus wants? What does he want more than anything else? Well, that's an easy one because he hasn't exactly kept it a secret. Jesus wants us to love him. In fact, he tells us that is the most important thing we can do with our lives. Love God! Jesus is God. He is saying, "Love me! The most important and highest thing you can do with your life is to love me!"

Although Jesus has planted desires and dreams in our hearts, he doesn't give first place to the use of our gifts to further the kingdom of God or to minister to his beloved lambs. Jesus says that the greatest command is to love him.

We love him by loving others, yes, but God gives first place to loving him, and we do that simply by being with him, spending time with him, fixing our gaze on who he is.

Now think about this: You are made in God's image, right? Down to your feminine core, you express something about the heart of God to the world. And what does every woman's heart long for? To be loved. To be chosen. To be a priority to someone. Think of how deeply this runs in you. Now you know something central about the heart of God. He wants that too.

Voluntarily offering our love to God is the most important thing we can do. Loving Jesus is the fire that fuels every other good work in our lives. And loving God enables us to live a courageous life that can't help but spill out onto others.

I choose to love God today. It's the most important choice I can make!

sitting at Jesus's feet

Mary … sat at the Lord's feet listening to what he said.
—Luke 10:39

Now to a story of two women: one who was distracted and one who couldn't take her eyes off Jesus.

> Jesus and his disciples … came to a village where a woman named Martha opened her home to him. She had a sister called Mary, who sat at the Lord's feet listening to what he said. But Martha was distracted by all the preparations that had to be made. She came to him and asked, "Lord, don't you care that my sister has left me to do the work by myself? Tell her to help me!"

> "Martha, Martha," the Lord answered, "you are worried and upset about many things, but few things are needed—or indeed only one. Mary has chosen what is better, and it will not be taken away from her." (Luke 10:38–42)

Martha criticized her sister and rebuked the Lord. "Why are you just sitting there? Do you not see what is going on here? I am working so hard, and my sister is doing nothing. Make her help me." I love how Jesus gently corrected Martha for her worry and distraction. He didn't say that what Martha was doing was wrong but that her attitude was. (Probably a good clue that we may be off in our attitudes is when we feel compelled to rebuke God for not intervening!)

But Mary's focus was undivided. She wasn't running about helping her sister because she was smitten with Jesus. She had chosen to learn from Jesus, to listen to his words, to open her heart and her mind to him. She was doing the one thing that was required—loving Jesus. And Jesus applauded her choice.

Mary sat at Jesus's feet, which is the sign of a disciple. (I love how Jesus treated women! It was scandalous at that time to have a woman disciple. But Jesus had them. He esteemed women.) Rather than being busy doing things for him, Mary was simply being with him. And Jesus said that being with him, listening to him, and honoring him with her attention and adoration was far above doing things for him.

You know that when you really love someone, it gives you great joy just to be in the same room with them. Our sons no longer live at home, and when they do come home for a visit, I am so happy! Just to have them under the same roof with me makes me glad. My heart rests in the joy of their proximity. You know this. Mary knew this. Jesus knows this too.

Jesus, I sit at your feet right now. What joy to think that my presence with you makes you happy! What do you want me to hear from you today?

when God lingers

Now Jesus loved Martha and her sister and Lazarus.
So, when he heard that Lazarus was ill, he stayed
two days longer in the place where he was.

—John 11:5–6 ESV

When Jesus heard that his good friend Lazarus was dying, he didn't rush to Lazarus's side. He had something even better in mind. So he waited where he was. And then he performed one of the greatest miracles of his earthly ministry and raised Lazarus from the dead.

Just as we have to do so often, Lazarus's sisters had to wait for God to come, realizing he wasn't going to come at the time they wanted.

Believing God is good in the midst of waiting is incredibly hard. Believing God is good in the midst of immense sorrow, loss, or pain is even more difficult. Those are the times that test our faith, transforming it to gold. What we come to know of God and the terrain he comes to inhabit in our hearts through trials leads people to say, "I wouldn't change a thing." That's the crazy, supernatural realm of God.

I know that many times God didn't answer your prayers in the way you wanted or in the timing you wanted. That was what Mary experienced when Jesus did not come and Lazarus died. Yet when Mary saw Jesus coming, she ran to him and fell at his feet. She worshipped him. She brought to Jesus the whole truth of who she was, including her profound grief and uncontrolled weeping. And in seeing her weeping, Jesus cried too.

Your tears move Jesus. Your waiting. Your love. Your sorrows. He is moved when you worship him even though it all looks hopeless. It is one of the deepest ways you can express your love for him. And one of the greatest times for him to show his love for you.

Jesus, I am waiting on you today. I have been waiting on you for a long time to come and heal certain areas of my life. And in the waiting, I worship you. I love you. I believe that you see me and will come soon to bring new life. In Jesus's name, amen.

72

---

lavish love

*Then Mary took about a pint of pure nard, an
expensive perfume; she poured it on Jesus' feet and
wiped his feet with her hair. And the house was
filled with the fragrance of the perfume.*

—John 12:3

Days after Jesus rose Lazarus from the dead, he was having
dinner with his friends. That's when Mary did the unthink-
able. She came into the room with an alabaster jar of very
expensive perfume. (Many commentators believe this perfume was her life savings.) Mary broke the neck of the jar
open and slowly poured some of the perfume on Jesus's head
and then poured the rest on his feet. Then she did something extremely intimate and scandalous. She unbound her
hair and wiped his feet with it, even though a respectable
woman did not let down her hair in public.

The fragrance of Mary's offering filled the room. There was a *change in the atmosphere*. When we pour out all we have in worship to Jesus, others around us sense the beauty of that offering.

But the Gospels tell us that those present that evening were indignant and rebuked her harshly. "What a waste of money! A whole year's wages poured out for nothing! Think of how many poor families could eat for a week on that."

Have you ever had your motives misunderstood? Have you ever had someone criticize the way you worship or spend your time or money, the way you minister or believe or come through or don't come through? Jesus knows well that it hurts to be misunderstood and judged. He knows it is part of the sorrow of living in a fallen world.

Jesus always defends a worshipper, and that night he defended Mary's reckless devotion. Jesus "got" Mary, and he "gets" you. He understood her heart and the depth of her love. She had her unique portion, true to her, and she gave it all.

Mary ministered to Jesus in a way that no one else even comprehended, because she knew him. She trusted him. She worshipped him lavishly.

And Jesus *loved* it.

Jesus, I want to worship you today with the abandon and intimacy that Mary had when she poured perfume on your feet. I want to worship you lavishly! Amen.

73

---

you are chosen

For he chose us in him before the creation of the
world to be holy and blameless in his sight.

—Ephesians 1:4

Growing up, I wasn't athletic. I was never picked first for
the team, and I was never once asked to a dance. When I
was in the fourth grade, however, my classmates chose me
to be Citizen of the Year. I still remember the joy of it. Each
day throughout the year, our teacher chose one student to
be Citizen of the Day. Their name went up on the special
chart for all to see. On the last day of school, the teacher
tallied up the names to see who had won the honor most
often. It turned out to be a tie between me and a cute boy
named Bobby. So she took a private vote. There were more
boys in the classroom than girls, so I was pretty certain I
wouldn't win. But I had an edge. My family was moving in a

week from our home in Prairie Village, Kansas, to unknown California. I was leaving, and everyone knew it. This could be my good-bye present. And I did win.

I didn't really care why I won. I simply cared that *I* was chosen. My prize was a certificate and the cardboard sheet with the school photos of all my classmates. I took their photos off the board, put them in an envelope, and brought them with me to California.

That was the spring immediately before what would become the earthquake of my young life. When we got to our new state, my family utterly fell apart. How many times did I go to my little box, pour over my classmates' pictures, and remember that I was loved? That I had been chosen? It was a God-given lifeline of remembrance when I needed it most.

Did you know that God chooses *you*? He chooses you to be in relationship with him. He chooses you to know his peace. He chooses you to receive his salvation.

When your world shakes and crumbles, remember this truth: you are chosen. Nothing will ever change that.

Jesus, I love that you have reached for me. Not for who I wish you had made me to be or who I yearn to be someday, but just for me, now, in my messiness, in the process of you transforming me! Amen.

74

---

a divine exchange

Teach me your ways, O LORD,
that I may live according to your truth!
Grant me purity of heart,
so that I may honor you.
With all my heart I will praise you, O Lord my God.
I will give glory to your name forever,
for your love for me is very great.

—Psalm 86:11–13 NLT

One of the best ways to remember who our God is and who
we are to him is to worship him. In worship, when we turn
the gaze of our hearts away from ourselves and our needs and
onto Jesus, a divine shift happens that brings a great good
to our lives. Our enormous struggles and concerns become
much less overwhelming in the face of our powerful, loving

Jesus. In worship, we remember that we have been bought with his precious blood. We remember who we belong to.

You are Jesus's beloved: "I belong to my beloved, and his desire is for me" (Song of Songs 7:10). He cares for you and those you love, beyond telling. You are forever loved.

Worshipping God is our response to being loved, forgiven, and known. It is our chance to offer our thanks for being seen, chosen, wanted, understood, cherished, and made new! Worship is our response to seeing Jesus as he really is: worthy, beautiful, endlessly good, kind, forgiving, generous, wonderful, and utterly and completely *for* us.

Worship is an encounter with God that changes us by aligning our spirits with truth even when it doesn't *feel* true. We pour ourselves out onto him, and he pours himself into us. It is a divine exchange that ministers to his heart and renews our own.

Intimate worship is simply telling God how wonderful he is and why. It is pouring out our love onto him like oil. We bring him all that we are as women, even our weariness and sorrow. In our loving of Jesus, we become increasingly available for him to continue his deep work in us, transforming us into the women we long to be.

Jesus, I give you my weariness. I give you my doubt. I give you my desire to give up. I come with my thirst. I offer you my desire, my gifting, my weakness, my need, my failure, my everything. I give you all that I am, God. I give you my love.

"she was with Jesus"

Whom have I in heaven but you?
And earth has nothing I desire besides you.
My flesh and my heart may fail,
but God is the strength of my heart
and my portion forever.
—Psalm 73:25–26

Our worship of Jesus pushes back the kingdom of darkness and ushers in the kingdom of God. It changes the atmosphere around us so that others can sense, *She was with Jesus.*

Why don't you take a few minutes and come before him now? Imagine you are sitting at his feet and listening, or washing his feet with your tears, or gazing up at him on the cross, or even bowing before the very much alive and risen Lord. There is no doing this wrong. It makes God so happy when we pause in the midst of our day or create an extended time alone with him simply to adore him!

Jesus is worthy of our devotion and thanks. Your Jesus is the One who rode into the depths of the darkest, most dangerous dungeon to rescue his true love. He is the One who will ride again on a white steed, with fire in his eyes and a flaming sword in his hand. He has inscribed you into the palm of his nail-pierced hand. He knows your every thought, numbers your every hair, and cherishes your every tear. Jesus weeps for you and with you, longs for you, hopes for you, dreams of you, and rejoices over you with singing. He is the One who has battled all the forces of hell to free you and who battles still.

Jesus is your knight in shining armor. He is the love you have been longing for. He is your dream come true. He is your hero. He is Aslan, the Lion of Judah, and the Lamb of God. He is the Prince of Peace, the Alpha and Omega, the First and the Last, the King of Kings and the Lord of Lords, the Mighty One.

His name is like a kiss and an earthquake. His gaze is on you. He has pledged his love to you and betrothed you to him forever. He is unchangeable, and his love will never fail you.

How will you respond? Love him. Adore him. Worship him.

God, who do I have in heaven but you? And earth has nothing I desire besides you. My flesh and my heart may fail, but you are the strength of my heart and my portion forever.

76

---

choose to believe

*Now the one who has fashioned us for this very
purpose is God, who has given us the Spirit as
a deposit, guaranteeing what is to come.*

—2 Corinthians 5:5

As women growing in our own becoming, we want to live with holy intention. We want to be awake to the present moment, to those around us, to the Spirit within us, and to our own souls. We are meant to live lives of significance. It is right that we desire to live for a purpose higher than having a clear complexion and being well liked. We want to live unto a high calling and a meaningful purpose, and that purpose flows out of our identity.

Knowing who we are enables us to live the life we have been born to live—the life the seen and unseen worlds need us to live. We need to know who we are and own who we are. Who *are* you? What is your identity—*really*?

203

You are a new creation in Christ, more than a conqueror. Victorious. Strong. Empowered. Safe. Secure. Sealed. You are a channel of the life and love of God. You are alive in Christ. You are the beloved of God. You are his.

Who is Jesus? He is the love you have been looking for all your life, and he has never taken his eyes off you. He has a name for you that he wants you to fully become; he holds your true identity, and this is what you are meant to grow into. So you'll want to ask Jesus your true name (or names—he often has several for us). As he tells you, dear one, choose to believe.

Jesus, I choose to believe that I am your beloved and that your desire is for me. I choose to believe that I am no longer forsaken or deserted but that I am your delight, sought after and dearly loved. Jesus, I want to become the woman you have in mind for me to be. Show me who she is; show me who I really am, who I was always meant to be. Tell me my true name; give me an image of who you see me becoming. Give me eyes to see and ears to hear and the courage to accept what you are saying. Tell me, Jesus.

what the world needs now

Seek ye first the kingdom of God, and his righteousness;
and all these things shall be added unto you.

—Matthew 6:33 KJV

We will never be happy as long as we are trying to live apart from ourselves or in disregard of ourselves, our hearts, our desires, our aches. Though happiness is never the highest goal, it comes to us naturally when the other aspects of our lives are in order.

Love is always the highest goal. Love of God, of others, and of ourselves, of the woman God has created us to be. We don't want to live in spite of ourselves, but we want to embrace ourselves, owning the multifaceted, mysterious women we are and the unique way we bring Jesus to the world.

You are the only you there has ever been or ever will be.

God made you *you* on purpose. Now. For a reason.

The world does not need yet another young woman who despises the lovely creation that she is. God does not long for another girl who rejects herself and, by extension, him. The world needs a woman who is thankful for how God has made her, who trusts that he is transforming her, and who actually enjoys who she is. It's a good thing to like who you are. God likes you! We get to like ourselves too. When you like yourself, you are free to enjoy others, and in your presence people experience an invitation to become and enjoy who they truly are as well.

Ask God, *How do you see me, God? Please give me your vision of the woman I am to become.* And then write it down. Write down what you hear from God or merely what, by faith, you choose to believe is becoming true for you because you want it to be!

daughter of the king

*For now we see only a reflection as in a mirror; then
we shall see face to face. Now I know in part; then
I shall know fully, even as I am fully known.*

—1 Corinthians 13:12

I confess I have a bit of a crush on Llywelyn the Great. This Prince of Wales was the first to truly unite his country, and much of his life is a picture of Jesus to me. I don't know why Hollywood has not made a movie about him, but they should. (Have your people call my people!)

Anyway, he was a nobleman whose grandson and namesake—known as Llywelyn the Last—followed in his grandfather's footsteps and tried to unite, lead, and protect Wales. His life is a noble story as well, but a sad one. He was killed in a small skirmish and was unable to save his country from the English invasion that changed the little country's destiny.

Llywelyn the Last had one heir—a baby girl. She was only months old when Wales fell to the English, but since she was an infant and a female, her fate was not as bad as it would have been had she been a boy. She was captured by King Edward's troops, and the king interned her at Sempringham Priory in England for the rest of her life. She eventually became a nun in her thirties and died twenty years later, knowing little of her heritage and speaking none of her native language. Her name was Gwenllian. She was a princess in exile, living in a land ruled by her father's enemy.

The Welsh have a word for the ache in one's heart for one's true home, for the longing that goes deeper than understanding: *hiraeth*. Gwenllian lived with that ache. She was meant to reign, but her throne was stolen. She was stripped of her authority and lived her life in captivity, never knowing her true identity, never hearing her true name. Would it have made a difference for Gwenllian if she had known the truth? Would it have mattered in her life, in her heart, if she had known who her father was? Who she was?

Does it make a difference in our lives to know our true identity? Oh yes. It makes all the difference in the world. Let us, then, remember who we truly are. Let us go further up and further in to all the riches and joy and intimacy and healing that God has for us!

What difference does it make in your life today to know that God, the King, is your Father?

---

never forget who you are

I will betroth you to me forever;
I will betroth you in righteousness and justice,
in love and compassion.
I will betroth you in faithfulness,
and you will acknowledge the LORD.

—Hosea 2:19–20

Do you remember who you are? Whose you are?

First, **you are the daughter of the King**. You are your Father's delight. You are the apple of his eye and the one on whom his affections rest.

Second, **you are the bride of Christ**. You are engaged to the High Prince. You are the beloved of Jesus. There is a royal wedding coming, unparalleled in the history of men and angels, and all the eyes of creation will be riveted and rejoicing.

Third, **you are the ally-friend of Jesus**. You were sent to this earth to bring about the invasion by his kingdom. You have a role in a mighty story filled with beauty and danger.

When we believe something is true, it affects the choices we make. We believe gravity exists, so we jump up, safe in the knowledge that we will come down again. We believe the sun will rise, so we go to bed without fear that night will last forever. But sometimes God calls us to believe something before we experientially know it. The popular saying is "seeing is believing," but in Christ, believing leads to seeing. God invites us to believe we are who he says we are: his beloved.

Jesus, I want to live out my identity today. I want to live as the princess I am!

what do you call yourself?

Do not call anything impure that God has made clean.

—Acts 10:15

What you name something is immeasurably important. What do you call yourself when you pass a mirror? When you make a mistake? When someone teases you?

There is power in what we name ourselves. There is power in what other people name us as well. Both the power to bless and the power to curse come from the heart and flow out of the mouth through words. What we call something and what we are called, whether good or evil, will play itself out in our lives.

A perfect real-life example of this took place in India several years ago. Nearly three hundred Indian girls gathered for a name-changing ceremony in India. Their names meant "unwanted" in Hindi, a reflection of the gender bias toward boys in India. But a central Indian district invited these girls to choose new names.

> The 285 girls—wearing their best outfits with barrettes, braids and bows in their hair—lined up to receive certificates with their new names along with small flower bouquets from Satara district officials in Maharashtra state.
>
> In shedding names like "Nakusa" or "Nakushi," which mean "unwanted" in Hindi, some girls chose to name themselves after Bollywood stars such as "Aishwarya." … Some just wanted traditional names with happier meanings, such as "Vaishali," or "prosperous, beautiful and good."
>
> "Now in school, my classmates and friends will be calling me this new name, and that makes me very happy," said a 15-year-old girl who had been named

Nakusa by a grandfather disappointed by
her birth.[1]

Isn't that a beautiful picture of redemption? We can
never forget that what we call ourselves—the words we use
to describe who we are, whether out loud or silently—is
powerful.

In Christ, I am no longer unclean; I have been cleansed.
I am no longer a sinner; I am a saint. I am no longer unwanted; I am sought after. I am no longer rejected; I am
pursued. I am no longer ugly; I am beautiful. I am no longer
guilty; I am blameless. I am no longer under condemnation;
I am innocent. I am no longer in bondage; I am free. I am
no longer alone; I am loved.

1   Chaya Babu, "285 Indian Girls Shed 'Unwanted' Names," Yahoo!
     News, October 22, 2011, http://news.yahoo.com/285-indian-girls
     -shed-unwanted-names-122551876.html.

81

---

he will change your name

And you will be given a new name by the LORD's own mouth.
—Isaiah 62:2 NLT

What other people call you affects your life, your relationships, and your walk with God. What you call yourself *affects your ability to become who you are meant to be.* God knows there is power in what we call ourselves. In light of this, listen to the fierce intention of God, who says he will change *your* name:

> Because I love [insert your name here],
>   I will not keep still.
> Because my heart yearns for [her],
>   I cannot remain silent.
>   I will not stop praying for her

until her righteousness shines like the
dawn,
and her salvation blazes like a burning
torch.
The nations will see your righteousness.
World leaders will be blinded by your
glory.
And you will be given a new name
by the LORD's own mouth.
The LORD will hold you in his hand for all
to see—
a splendid crown in the hand of God.
Never again will you be called "The
Forsaken City"
or "The Desolate Land."
Your new name will be "The City of God's
Delight"
and "The Bride of God,"
for the LORD delights in you
and will claim you as his bride.

(Isa. 62:1–4 NLT)

This beautiful passage comes after Isaiah 61, which promises your healing and restoration and your deliverance from the Enemy. Now God promises a new name. No longer will you be called Deserted but Sought After. You are pursued. You are worth pursuing, chasing after, romancing. You are wanted.

God wants us to name things correctly, including ourselves. It's vitally important that we do.

Pray this passage from Isaiah, inserting your name in the first verse.

82

you are the beloved

I belong to my beloved,
and his desire is for me.

—Song of Songs 7:10

God names you Beloved. What does *beloved* mean? It means one greatly loved, dear to the heart. It means admired, adored, cherished, darling. Beloved means dear, dear one, dearest, esteemed, favorite, honey. It means ladylove, light of love, loved one, lover, precious, prized, respected, and revered. *Beloved* means you. *It means who you are to him. And who you are to him means everything.*

God calls you to believe it. He wants you to know who you are. You need to. The fruit of knowing who you are to Christ is intimacy with him. It isn't walking around all puffed up. *Oh, look at me! I'm something special!* The fruit is neither pride nor arrogance. The fruit is humility. It is surrendered gratefulness. The fruit of believing we are who God says we are is a deepening love for Jesus. We love because he first loved us. Belief evokes a response; we choose to draw near to this God who prizes us. And that is exactly what God is after.

I belong to Jesus today and his desire is for me! I am his beloved and nothing will ever, ever change that.

83

focusing on faithfulness

Keep your eyes on Jesus, who both began
and finished this race we're in.

—Hebrews 12:2 MSG

So, who are you?

When we believe that our truest identity is a sinner, then we walk around ashamed, accused, condemned. Separated from God. Which does not make for a happy camper and which is exactly where our Enemy, the Devil, wants us to live. The Devil is called the accuser of the brethren for a reason.

When the focus of our hearts is solely on our failings, then our hearts spiral down. God tells us not to focus on our failings but on his faithfulness. He calls us to gaze not on our brokenness but on our Healer. We move toward what we focus on.

Scripture warns us not to think more highly of ourselves than we ought. To be honest, I have yet to meet that woman who thinks of herself too highly. But I have met a lot of women who think much less of themselves than they ought. Certainly much less than God does. And that is not only disheartening; it is dangerous. Why? Because you cannot live well, you cannot love well, and you cannot fulfill your destiny if you do not know who you are.

You cannot become yourself if you do not know who you are to become.

Jesus, show me who you want me to become. I want to focus my eyes on the finish line—being completely who God made me to be, completely faithful, completely living out my identity as your beloved! You have run this race too, so you know what it is like. Run alongside me so that I might live well and love well, to the glory of your name. Amen.

84

"scoreboard."

For the accuser of our brothers and sisters,
who accuses them before our God day and night,
has been hurled down.

—Revelation 12:10

My friend's son Gannon is a superb soccer player. As a freshman in high school, he helped lead the varsity team to the state championship. He is a quiet, polite young man who transforms into a warrior once he hits the field.

During one of his recent games, Gannon's team was in the lead by three goals, a massive lead in soccer. Guarding Gannon was a player who used insults to try to keep Gannon from being his glorious soccer-playing self. They call it "talking smack": "You are the worst player on this team." "You can't even kick the ball." "No one on your team likes you." "You're just a baby freshman." "Go home, little boy."

Gannon's accuser didn't take a break. Gannon said it was the most difficult thing he had ever endured on the field. "You missed! You are always going to miss." Accusations hurt.

But Gannon didn't engage his accuser in a verbal battle. He didn't entertain the accusations coming against him or defend himself. He merely answered him, "Scoreboard." That is all he ever replied. "Scoreboard." His accuser could say what he wanted, but Gannon's team was winning the game. He and his teammates were playing well. Gannon's defense lay in the truth. You bet they won that game. And that silenced his accuser.

Do you ever hear accusing words about yourself—not from someone else but from inside you? *You're blowing it. You can't do this well at all. You never will. You're not qualified. You don't have any real friends. You should just go home.* What do you hear when you find out you weren't invited to a party? When you get a bad grade on a test or find out you didn't get the job you wanted?

The next time you hear the Accuser's voice, remind him, "Scoreboard." Jesus has won your victory, and you are victorious in him. Sin, failure, or your past does not define you. You are forever and only defined by the finished work of Jesus Christ. You are a daughter. A bride. And you are beautiful.

I do not need to hear or believe accusing words about who I am from anyone (including me!), because Jesus has already defeated my accuser, Satan. Only the finished work of Jesus Christ defines who I am!

85

---

your truest identity

Resist the devil, and he will flee from you.
—James 4:7 ESV

I grew up believing I was fat and ugly. I believed I could never be good enough—and I told myself that every day.

When we believe that our truest identity is a sinner, we walk around ashamed. We tell ourselves we are ugly, unwanted failures. That's exactly where our Enemy, the Devil, wants us to live. The Devil is called the Accuser for a reason.

Your thoughts about yourself affect your ability to become who you were meant to be. Though the author is unknown, I love the following quote. It helps me realize there are tangible ramifications to my thoughts. They matter. They have an effect.

Watch your thoughts, for they
become words.

Watch your words, for they
become actions.
Watch your actions, for they
become habits.
Watch your habits, for they
become your character.
And watch your character, for it
becomes your destiny!
What we think, we become.

What we think, we become. What are you thinking about your-self today?

86

you make him happy

I am my beloved's, and my beloved is mine.

—Song of Solomon 6:3 KJV

In the midst of your day—in the mess, the mundane, the glorious—when you laugh and live well and when you don't, get into the habit of stopping and asking yourself, *What am I thinking is true about myself?* If it does not line up with the Word of God, reject it as a lie. Replace it with the truth.

What would it be like right now to entertain the possibility in your heart that all God says about you is true?

You are his delight.

You make him happy just by being you.

He thinks you're lovely.

You are his beloved.

You are the one who has captured his heart.

What difference would it make in your life if these things really were true? Think of it. Let your heart go there for a moment. Because it does make all the difference in the world—and it really is true!

Ask God, *Am I your beloved? How do you see me? Do you delight in me? Do you love me because you're God and that's your job, or do you love me simply for me?*

You, dear heart, you *are* the beloved.

Jesus, thank you for this truth about me. I receive it. I agree with you, and I declare that I am your daughter. I am chosen, holy, and dearly loved. I am the apple of your eye. I am your beloved, and your desire is for me. Please write this truth deep in my heart. In Jesus's name I pray. Amen.

87

---

call it good

Create in me a pure heart, O God,
and renew a steadfast spirit within me.

—Psalm 51:10

Have you ever had to go to an event you didn't want to go to, a party or game or family gathering? I had a birthday party I needed to attend recently, and I wasn't very happy about it. I complained to my husband that I had to go and spend hours with people I had never met and would never see again. Blah-blah-blah. And John said, "Rename it. Call it good."

Right—it's not evil; it's good. It's an opportunity to bless someone I care very much about. It's a chance to celebrate her life. I renamed it, changed my frame of reference, and went with a happy heart.

There are many things we need to rename in our lives. Our school experience. Our relationships. Even our life itself. Rename them. Rename your life. It's good because your life belongs to our good God, and he's got you. Rename yourself. *God has.*

My parents named me Stasi. It means resurrection. There is a lot in my life that has needed resurrecting over the years—my wounded heart, my damaged sexuality, my broken self-perception, my dreams, my relationships, my calling. And God is resurrecting every area of my life to *life*. He is resurrecting my mind to be able to believe that all he has made—including all he has made *me*—is good. He is resurrecting my dreams and my desires and even my yearning to be deeply known and perfectly loved. Yes, my parents named me Stasi, but really it was God who named me Resurrection. And it's good!

Jesus, what are you calling me to rename in my life today? What am I calling evil that you want to redeem so I can call it good?

88

what has God named you?

It stands to reason, doesn't it, that if the alive-and-present God who raised Jesus from the dead moves into your life, he'll do the same thing in you that he did in Jesus, bringing you alive to himself? When God lives and breathes in you (and he does, as surely as he did in Jesus), you are delivered from that dead life. With his Spirit living in you, your body will be as alive as Christ's!

—Romans 8:10–11 MSG

Do you know what your given name means? It's a good idea to find out. If you don't like the meaning you initially discover, press in to find out more about it. Ask God to reveal to you why he named you what he did.

A friend of mine's name is Melanie. I asked her what it means, and with a little shrug she told me, "It means dark." Huh. Dark. We pressed in to find out more about what her name means and discovered it doesn't simply mean "dark." It means "dark beauty." In Hebrew it actually means "grace-filled beauty." Song of Songs says, "Dark am I, yet lovely" (1:5). Which can mean, "Yes, I am imperfect, and I see my many failings and sins, but when God looks at me, he sees my beauty, not my sin. To Jesus, I am and have only ever been lovely." That's what Melanie means. See, it's a good idea to find out.

Because whatever else is true about what you are named, God says, *No longer are you called desolate, but married. No longer are you alone or unseen; your name is Sought After. Beloved. Mine. No longer are you called unwanted. Your name is good.*

How do you feel about your name? What does your name mean? (If you're not sure, look it up on a baby name site online.) Ask God to reveal to you the spiritual significance behind your name.

never alone

*Now to him who is able to keep you from stumbling
and to present you blameless before the presence of his
glory with great joy, to the only God, our Savior, through
Jesus Christ our Lord, be glory, majesty, dominion, and
authority, before all time and now and forever.*

—Jude 24–25 ESV

Each and every one of us is still growing into the woman we
want to be, the woman God created us to be. Our life is one
of continual discovery and transformation.

You have so many experiences ahead of you! Choices
to make. Truths to believe. And so much to learn. I'm still
learning too. We are on this road together, urged on by a
great company of witnesses, seen and unseen. We are surrounded by love every moment of our lives. We are held
in the gaze of the One who has won everything, done

everything, and paid everything so that we might be free to live, free to love, and free to be ourselves. We are free to offer all that we are back to him in a life rich with joy, steeped in goodness, strengthened in hope, and abounding in love.

Jesus goes before you, behind you, and within you. You are never alone, and you will always have all you need.

Let's press on together.

Lord, I want to change [this area of my life], and I am willing to make whatever changes are needed in order to fulfill your plan for me in this area. I am willing to see things your way. Please show me, lead me, guide me. In Jesus's name, amen.

90

---

more joy ahead

The Lord bless you
and keep you;
the Lord make his face shine on you
and be gracious to you;
the Lord turn his face toward you
and give you peace.

—Numbers 6:24–26

I know you are a young woman who wants her life to be one of power and significance. You want to live with holy intention, becoming all you are meant to be, and to partner with Jesus in bringing his kingdom.

Here are a few reminders about how God sees you right now:

- You are deeply and completely loved (Rom. 8:38–39).
- You are totally and completely forgiven (1 John 2:12).
- When God sees you, he sees the righteousness of Jesus (2 Cor. 5:21).
- You mean the whole world to him (John 3:16).
- He thinks you are beautiful (Song of Songs 4:1).
- He is committed to your restoration (Rom. 8:29).
- You are not now, nor have you ever been, alone (Heb. 13:5).

Know that you are not alone, friend. You are being prayed for and cheered on by a great company of witnesses, including me. Your life is well underway. You are growing in the knowledge that God is the key to living the life you were meant to live. There is more of life to be had. There is more healing, more freedom, and more adventure!

You are loved. You are beautiful. And there is much joy ahead.

God, I praise you because I am fearfully and wonderfully made. I want to know the healing, freedom, and adventure you have for me!

a few final words from stasi

God has revealed both himself and yourself to you in this book. Now it's time to flex your faith muscles and choose to believe him in the moments when you are *feeling* beloved, beautiful, and accepted and in the moments when you are not.

The more we know Jesus, the more we love him. The more we love him, the more healed and the more ourselves we become. People will ask you for the reason for the hope that is within you! Jesus is the reason. He is so marvelous, and there is no end to discovering the beauty and majesty of his alluring heart. So let the adventure continue. We're in it together!

Another Book from
Stasi Eldredge

You might sometimes feel inadequate in the world's eyes, but the truth is, you are beautiful, valuable, and made with a purpose! Discover the truth with Stasi.

A Gift to You:

We'd like to give you the first 2 chapters of Stasi's book *Free to Be Me*…

Because we know a girl's teenage years can be extremely challenging. Stasi's message will allow these girls to see the hand of God in their story and trust Him with their hopes and desires.

To get your two free chapters, please visit **http://bit.ly/free-to-be-me**